Michael Jackson: The King of Pop's DARKEST HOUR

by
LISA D. CAMPBELL
Foreword by
BOB JONES

BRANDEN PUBLISHING COMPANY, Inc.
Boston

Library of Congress Cataloging-in-Publication Data

Campbell, Lisa D.
    Michael Jackson : the king of pop's darkest hour /
by Lisa D. Campbell.
       p. cm.
    Includes bibliographical references and index.
    ISBN 0-8283-2003-9 :
    1. Jackson, Michael, 1958-   .
    2. Rock musicians--United States--Biography.
     I. Title.
ML420.J175C33 1994
782.42166'092--dc20
[B]   94-29341
                         CIP
                         MN

BRANDEN PUBLISHING COMPANY
17 Station Street
Box 843 Brookline Village
Boston, MA 02147

While 1993 started out to be banner year for Michael Jackson, it later turned out to be a very painful and immensely difficult period for him. Many seemed to turn away from him when he needed them most. Some of his closet friends were conspicuously silent, the media wouldn't let up in their relentless search for scandal, former employees, and even a certain member of his family, were eager to turn on him for a quick buck. There were those however that stood steadfastly by Michael Jackson throughout this whole ugly mess, his millions of devoted fans. I wish to take this opportunity to thank all of his fans for their unwavering support. Special thanks also to everyone who publicly supported Michael Jackson, including the following:

James Alsop, Jeremy Alsop, Florence Anthony, Lori Byler, Johnnie Cochran Jr., Frank Dileo, Sandy Gallin, Berry Gordy, Adrian Grant, Jackie Jackson, Janet Jackson, Jermaine Jackson, Joseph Jackson, Katherine Jackson, Randy Jackson, Rebbie Jackson, Tito Jackson, John H. Johnson and Robert Johnson of *Jet Magazine*, Quincy Jones, Jerry Kramer, MTV, Paul McCartney, Majestik Magnificent, Steve Manning, Carole Nowicki, Michael Peters, Amanda Porter, Shannon Reeves of the NAACP, Alfonso Ribeiro, Teddy Riley, Audrey Ruttan, Maximilian Schell, Liz Smith, Sony Music, Bruce Swedien, J. Randy Taraborrelli, Tatiana Thumbtzen, Raul Velasco, Howard Weitzman, Jeanne White-Ginder, DeWayne Wickman, Norman Winter, and Stevie Wonder.

And very deepest gratitude to the one person who showed Michael the depths of her friendship and trust, the best friend Michael could ever hope for, Miss Elizabeth Taylor.

This book is dedicated with admiration, love, and respect to the King of Pop, Michael Joseph Jackson. You make the world a better place.

"Don't let nobody take you down"

Keep The Faith

Glen Ballard
Siedah Garrett
Michael Jackson

S pecial thanks to everyone who helped me in completing this book. I appreciate your love, encouragement, and understanding in what was a difficult and painful time for me, watching someone I care very much for, and feel very close to, endure such pain and persecution.

John, thank you for your help, understanding, and encouragement. I love you.

Mom and Dad, thank you for your continued confidence in me, I love you.

Michele, this is the best restaurant I've ever eaten in. Truly, I couldn't have done this without your immeasurable amount of help. Thank you so much.

CONTENTS

FOREWORD

Michael Jackson first became aware of Lisa Campbell's work with the publication of *Michael Jackson: The King of Pop*, in 1993, when he received a copy of the book at my office. He is impressed with her work and greatly appreciates the painstaking measures taken for accuracy. We are equally pleased to now have the opportunity to contribute this Foreword for this new volume.

Lisa has presented here a fair overview of the events that took place when Michael became the victim of false and cruel allegations, and the irresponsible persecution he suffered at the hands of the media. We have long been the victims of rumors and lies through the media but nothing could have prepared us for that to which he was recently subjected.

Michael experienced pain and humiliation to a depth he never realized existed. The tremendous distress he suffered during this period had profound effects on him both emotionally and physically. He has now overcome those difficulties with knowledge of his complete innocence and his deep faith in God.

Michael has come through the experience a stronger person due largely to his faith and the incredible amount of support received from his friends and fans throughout the world. The underlying love and support he received from the fans and their refusal to believe the worst truly touched his heart.

His goal is to spread pure and simple love around the world. Children are his greatest source of joy. That is a part of him which will not ever change.

Michael knows that his fans suffered with him and shared in his pain. He is deeply grateful for all of the love he has received.

He loves you all.

BOB JONES
Vice President
Michael J. Jackson Productions

1

MICHAEL TALKS

Nineteen hundred ninety three started out to be one of the best years ever for Michael Jackson. His latest release, *Dangerous,* was still selling steadily around the world, well over a year after its release. "Heal the World", the sixth single released from *Dangerous*, was just entering the pop and R&B singles charts. The Dangerous tour was scheduled to begin a set of Asian dates in late summer with money raised at each stop going to the Heal the World Foundation. Of course, there were lots and lots of awards to be accepted, records to set, and "firsts" to achieve, in other words, it was business as usual for Michael Jackson. More significantly, Michael Jackson would finally begin an attempt to shed his media shy image, becoming more accessible to the media and the public. No one could have ever guessed the year would take such a startling twist and end on such a disturbing, painful, note.

Michael participated in two festivities celebrating the inauguration of President Bill Clinton. First, he joined several other celebrities, including Diana Ross, on the steps of the Lincoln Memorial the afternoon of January 18 to sing "We Are the World" for a pre-inaugural celebration. The crowd cheered wildly as Michael, dressed in black and gold, ascended the steps to the stage. The celebrities were soon joined by the new first family, with Michael Jackson standing between President elect Bill Clinton and his daughter Chelsea.

That very evening, Michael found himself picking up honors at the 25th Annual NAACP Image Awards. "Black or White" was named as the Best Music Video. In accepting the award Michael was greeted with a standing ovation, he said he was very surprised, that he really didn't expect to win. Michael was also named as the recipient of the NAACP Image Award for Entertainer of the Year. A video tribute to Michael Jackson was capped off by Patti Labelle and the Voices of Faith Choir singing "Will You Be There". The award was presented to Michael by actor Wesley Snipes who had played the role of a gang member in the video for "Bad". Michael was seated in the front row of the audience with his mother, Katherine, and his longtime security chief, Bill Bray, and Bob Jones, Vice President of MSS Productions.

The next day, Michael was among the performers taking part in *An American Reunion: The 52nd Presidential Inaugural Gala*. Of the many performers taking part in the show, only two performed more than one quick number, Clinton friend and supporter Barbra Streisand, and the King of Pop. Michael first addressed President elect Clinton on the need for increased funding for AIDS research. He then sang "Gone Too Soon", his anthem for his friend who lost his life to AIDS, Ryan White. Michael was soon surrounded on stage by children for "Heal the World". To close the show, Michael joined the other performers on stage to join a specially reunited Fleetwood Mac in singing "Don't Stop (Thinking About Tomorrow)" which had become the theme song of the Clinton campaign.

Michael was collecting awards again on January 25 at the American Music Awards, where he had five nominations. *Dangerous* was voted as the Favorite Pop/Rock Album, and "Remember the Time" was chosen as the Favorite Soul/R&B Single. Besides these awards, Michael received a special honor, becoming the first recipient of the American Music Award International Artist Award. The award was presented by Elizabeth Taylor, and a taped message from Eddie Murphy revealed the award will in the future be named "The Michael Jackson International Artist Award."

The American Music Awards opened with a performance by the King of Pop himself. Machine gun fire sprays out and a dancer drops to his death as Michael Jackson is revealed standing behind him. Dressed in a dark pinstripe suit, spats, and fedora, Michael opened the show with "Dangerous". In accepting an offer from the show's executive producer, Dick Clark, to perform on the show, Michael asked if he could open the show, to which Clark responded, "Michael, you can do whatever you want." Clark added, "I couldn't think of anyone more appropriate to kick off our 20th anniversary show. Not only is Michael one of the most exciting stage performers in the business, but one of the most honored as well."

The day following the American Music Awards, Michael was preparing for his next public performance, which would be in less than one week. On January 27, he attended a press conference to accept donations to his Heal the World Foundation. Michael Jackson was to provide the halftime entertainment for the Super Bowl and in return, donations of $100,000 each were made by the NFL and Super Bowl sponsor Frito Lay. Michael was also presented with a custom Super Bowl jacket. Michael's agreement to perform at halftime of the Super Bowl was made on the condition that it be a benefit performance for his charity.

When Super Bowl Sunday, January 31, finally arrived Michael dazzled the fans at the Rosebowl and millions of television viewers with the most spectacular halftime show ever produced. His performance began similarly to his Dangerous tour performances, with Michael exploding onto the stage only to stand absolutely motionless while the crowd cheered out of control. He started off with "Jam", dressed all in black and gold performing meticulously timed and synchronized choreography with his back up dancers. Removing his black military jacket and adding a black fedora, he re-created an abbreviated version of his unforgettable performance of "Billie Jean" from *Motown 25*. An equally exciting performance of "Black or White" followed. Children then surrounded Michael on stage for "Heal the World" while a gigantic globe inflated from the center of the stage. Unveiling children's drawings made up of individual cards held up by each section of fans in the stands, Michael addressed the crowd briefly and performed "Heal the World". Michael Jackson, as usual, mesmerized his audience with a performance delivered with more energy than most people expend in a year.

Normally, during the halftime show of the Super Bowl, approximately 20% of the viewing audience is lost.

This year, the number of viewers tuning in increased by five million, attracting the largest TV audience in history. Approximately 133.4 million people in the U.S. tuned in to see the King of Pop, and he didn't disappoint. Dick Ebersol, President of NBC-TV Sports, also wasn't disappointed:

We extend to Michael Jackson our extreme appreciation for helping NBC capture the largest total audience in American television history. A significant factor in the ratings success was that Michael Jackson's performance held the audience at halftime. It was a great example of teamwork between the National Football League, Michael Jackson and NBC and we can all be happy with the results.

Michael's spellbinding halftime extravaganza was not lost on record buyers. In the two weeks following his Super Bowl performance, sales of *Dangerous* skyrocketed, rising an incredible ninety points on *Billboard's* pop album charts to number forty one. Just like his performance on *Motown 25,* his performance at the Super Bowl seemed to bring his music to a whole new audience.

Continuing his media blitz, it was announced that Michael Jackson had agreed to a live ninety minute interview with Oprah Winfrey. The interview was said to be Michael's idea, and he agreed to discuss anything, though he didn't want it to be one of those "look at how many cars he has" kind of thing. Oprah reportedly had lots of footage of Michael's career handy to help fill time in case Michael turned out not to be too talkative. It wasn't necessary though as Michael was eager to dispel the many falsehoods about him that have been circulated, and believed, for many years. He refused to answer only two questions. One asking for a response to some of the allegations made by LaToya in her book, to which Michael said he couldn't answer because he honestly hadn't read the book. The only other question he refused to answer was whether or not he was still a virgin, at which he became quite embarrassed, "How could you ask me that?", and said only "I'm a gentleman". He did allow however that he has been in love, twice, with Brooke Shields and "one other girl".

Michael Jackson Talks To...Oprah was broadcast live around the world from Michael's Neverland Valley Ranch. Among the many silly and ridiculous rumors he finally responded to were his reported efforts to buy the elephant man's bones, "Where am I going to put some bones?"; his desire to sleep in a hyperbaric chamber, calling it "one of those tabloid things, it's completely made up", not mentioning he started that story himself; and his proposal to Elizabeth Taylor. Taylor, who was with Michael at the time of the interview, came on camera to also deny that Michael had ever proposed to her and added that she never proposed to him either. She also described Michael as "the least weird man I've ever known... He is highly intelligent, shrewd, intuitive, understanding, sympathetic, generous, to almost a fault, of himself. If he has any eccentricities, it's that he is like larger than life and some people just cannot accept that or face it or understand it."

To those who believed he bleached his dark skin, he revealed that he actually suffers from a skin disorder that destroys the pigmentation of the skin. After finally saying that he is not aware of anything that can actually bleach skin, he revealed further that the stories that he bleached his skin because he did not want to be black or was ashamed to be black, hurt him, that the skin disorder was a problem for him and something he couldn't control. Makeup is used to help even out blotches that are caused on the skin. He pointed out that people don't think anything however, of someone who will sit in the sun for hours to change the color of their skin, to become something they are not.

Viewers weren't given a look at his cars, but he did offer a brief look at his amusement park, all lit up beautifully with thousands of tiny lights, and his private movie theater, complete with built in hospital beds for visiting children who are too ill to sit up. Michael's house and the rest of the grounds of the ranch, including his private zoo, were off limits.

Michael gave Oprah a quick moon-walking lesson on the stage in front of the giant movie screen, but not too much because, "I'm a little rusty." Michael's latest video for "Give in to Me" was then premiered on worldwide television from his own movie theater.

Michael Jackson Talks To... Oprah attracted 90 million viewers in the U.S., making it the fourth most watched, non sports, program in history. Approximately half of all television sets were tuned in to see the King of Pop. The interview was heavily hyped beforehand, and afterward was treated as a major news story, with every news program, newspaper and talk show now offering expert information on vitiligo, the skin disorder that Michael had described.

The public's reaction to Michael's candid responses during the interview only continued the drive up the charts for *Dangerous*. Within three weeks of the interview, *Dangerous* rose another thirty one points on the album charts and was now at number ten, well over a year after its release. *Billboard* magazine officials said they had never seen such a rebound on the charts. Sales and airplay of his current single, "Heal the World" also did a quick turn-a-round. The single, which had peaked at number fifty two and had begun dropping, went back up the pop singles chart to number twenty seven.

Dangerous was Michael Jackson's first album under his new multi-million dollar contract with Sony Music. Some speculated that if his future albums continued to sell as well as his previous efforts, the contract could generate a billion dollars in revenue for Sony. That looked to be very possible with *Dangerous.* During its first few months of release, in late 1991 and early 1992, it was selling at a faster pace than did *Thriller,* the biggest selling album of all time, and *Bad,* the second best selling album of all time. It looked like Michael Jackson could soon have the top three best selling albums of all time, the only question was in what order; *Thriller, Bad,* and *Dangerous?* Or *Thriller, Dangerous,* and *Bad?* With *Thriller* appearing on *Billboard's* Top Pop Catalog Albums chart, it would be a while before even Michael Jackson could top its sales.

While *Dangerous* was rising quickly on the album charts once again, a fellow Sony artist was fighting in court to get out of his contract with Sony. George Michael, who had had great success with his *Faith* album, felt Sony had taken advantage of him in his contract as it didn't measure up to the contracts of other Sony artists Michael Jackson, Bruce Springsteen, and Barbra Streisand. George Michael wanted to compare his contract with the contracts of these other artists. With one very successful album, it is doubtful that Sony considered George Michael to be in their league. Michael Jackson, the King of Pop, has had successful albums for CBS Records, later Sony Music, since the

1970's, not to mention recording the top two best selling albums of all time. The Boss, Bruce Springsteen, has been popular with the working class for just as long. Barbra Streisand, while not having a cute nickname, has had a string of successes over many years as well, and is widely regarded as a legend.

The Michael media blitz continued with his appearance at the 35th Annual Grammy Awards on February 24, where Janet Jackson presented the Grammy Legend Award to her big brother, Michael. After narrating a tribute to her brother, "How To Become A Legend", Janet brought Michael on stage from his front row seat at the Shrine Auditorium, "Now I'm very happy to present the Grammy Legend Award for 1993 to my big brother, Michael Jackson." Looking dashing in black jeans and boots, a white t-shirt and a white beaded jacket, Michael embraced Janet. Instead of performing on the show, as had been previously announced, Michael chose instead to speak. In his acceptance speech, which lasted an incredible four minutes, Michael poked fun at himself and showed his sense of humor that many haven't had an opportunity to see. Approaching the microphone, standing next to Janet and putting his arm around her, Michael remarked, "I hope this finally puts to rest another rumor that has been in the press for too many years...me and Janet really are two different people!" He brought more laughs from the crowd when he began, "In the past month I've gone from 'Where is he?' to 'Here he is again!'". His comments prompted host Garry Shandling to ask, "When did he get so damn funny?" The rest of Michael's comments centered on his feeling that it was "nice to be thought of as a person and not as a personality,...:

Because I don't read all the things written about me, I wasn't aware the world thought I was so weird and bizarre. But when you grow up as I did in front of 100 million people since the age of 5, you're automatically different. The last few weeks I have been cleansing myself and it has been a rebirth for myself, it's like a cleansing spirit. My childhood was completely taken away from me. There was no Christmas, no birthdays. It was not a normal childhood, no normal pleasures of childhood. Those were exchanged for hard work, struggle and pain, and eventual material and professional success. But as an awful price, I cannot recreate that part of my life. Nor would I change any part of my life. However, today when I create my music I feel like an instrument of nature. I wonder what delight nature feels when we open our hearts and express our God given talents. The sound of approval rolls across the universe and the whole world abounds in magic. Wonder fills our hearts for we have glimpsed for an instant the playfulness of life.

And that's why I love children and learn so much from being around them. I realize that many of the world's problems today, from inner city crime to large scale wars and terrorism and over crowded prisons are a result of the fact that children have had their childhoods stolen from them. The magic, the wonder, the mystery and the innocence of a child's heart are the seeds of creativity that will heal the world. I really believe that.

What we need to learn from children isn't childish. Being with them connects us to the deeper wisdom of life which is ever present and asks only to be lived. They know the way to solutions that lie trying to be recognized in our own hearts.

Today I would like to thank all the children of the world including the sick and deprived, I am so sensitive to your pain. I also want to thank all those who have helped me to channel my talents here on Earth. ˜ From the beginning, my parents, all my brothers and sisters, especially Janet. I am so proud of her, it's incredible. I remember when we were little I used to ask her to be Ginger Rogers while I was Fred Astaire. The Motown family, my teacher, ·Berry Gordy, Diana Ross, I love you. Suzanne de Passe, the wonderful, great Quincy Jones, Teddy Riley, my new godson Michael Gibb, my new Sony family Akio Morita, Mickey Schulhof, Tommy Mottola, Dave Glew, Polly Anthony, thanks for making one of my most creative efforts, the album **Dangerous** *such an incredible success. I love you all so much. Sandy Gallin, Jim Morey, all the fantastic fans around the world, I love you very much.*

Besides his honor as the Grammy Legend, Michael had two Grammy nominations. He was nominated for Best Pop Male Vocal for "Black or White" and for Best R&B Male Vocal for "Jam". The Pop Male Vocal award went to Eric Clapton for "Tears in Heaven" and the R&B Male Vocal Grammy went to Al Jarreau for "Heaven and Earth". Teddy Riley, who co-produced several tracks on *Dangerous* was nominated for Producer of the Year, but lost to Lindsey Buckingham and Vince Gill. The Grammy for Best Engineered Recording went to Bruce Swedian for *Dangerous*.

The new social butterfly and his date, Brooke Shields, attended Sony Music's party at Jimmy's in Beverly Hills along with Bob Jones and his date. They later made a brief appearance at the Polygram Label Group's party on the A&M movie lot following the awards. Michael's appearance at the party was said to be the "buzz" of the evening.

Eric Clapton's multi-Grammy winning song, "Tears in Heaven" was played at the funeral service of a two year old boy who was kidnapped and murdered in Liverpool, England, by two ten-year olds. Also played at the service was a song the boy reportedly loved to dance to, Michael Jackson's "Heal the World".

In the spring of 1993, it was announced that Michael Jackson had formed an independent film company dedicated to producing uplifting movies. Michael Jackson Productions, Inc., will donate a share of its profits to Michael's Heal the World Foundation. In a statement Michael said, "I believe passionately in the power of mass entertainment and have seen how, with positive messages, it can help alleviate the problems we face, including the suffering of the world's children."

Another project Michael was reported to be involved with, that is also dedicated to children, is a plan to form an entertainment and educational cable television network. Michael is partners in the venture with former junk bond king, Michael Milken.

Michael was also said to be involved in another video game for Sega/Genesis. Sega built its first Virtua-Land arcade in Las Vegas that includes large screen TV's, moving platforms, monitors, and 3-D videographics, with Michael Jackson's likeness used as the commander in an eight-player attack squad game.

The Rock & Roll Cookbook, by Dick and Sandy St. John, was published that includes recipes from various rock stars. Included in the book is a recipe for Maple Pecan Butter Cookies from Michael Jackson. It does not reveal however how often he makes these cookies, or if he wears just one oven mitt.

Within just a few years of being marketed, figurines of Michael Raisin had dramatically increased in value. The figurines were taken from California Raisin commercials Michael contributed to in which a raisin figure was modeled after him. The figurines, which initially sold for $2.99, were now listed in *U.S. Toy Trader* and *Toy Shop Collectible* publications as the rarest of the California Raisin collectibles. Their values were now listed as ranging between $35 and $100.

The first weekend of March was declared Michael Jackson Weekend once again on MTV. The music network featured a special countdown of Michael Jackson videos, a sneak peak at his latest video for "Who Is It", and the MTV premiere of the video for "Give in to Me". Michael Jackson specials *Live and Dangerous, Moonwalker*, and *Making Michael Jackson's Thriller* were also broadcast during the weekend.

The video for "Who Is It" is a composite of earlier videos and performances. The song was released by Epic as Michael's next single as a last minute replacement for "Give in to Me", in reaction to the overwhelming public response to Michael's brief a cappella performance of the song during his interview with Oprah Winfrey. In fact, a bit of Michael's performance of the song from the interview was included on the cassette single. "Who Is It" peaked at number fourteen on the pop singles chart and at number six on the R&B chart.

"Who Is It" was the subject of an MTV contest which invited viewers to make a video for Michael's song. The 3,700 entries were narrowed down to ten then submitted to Michael to choose the three finalists. Each finalist won a trip for two to Neverland Valley. The winner was awarded $10,000 and a chance to direct a video for CBS. Eddie Barber, Bill Green, and J. Randall Argue were the finalists that were invited to the ranch, and their video entries were shown during MTV's

"My Weekend at Neverland Valley" June 26 and 27, 1993.

Michael had three nominations and received the Humanitarian of the Year award at the Seventh Annual Soul Train Awards that were handed out in March. Despite having sprained his ankle the day before during dance rehearsals, he attended the awards presentation and he performed as scheduled.

His first nomination was for Best R&B/Soul Music Video for "Remember the Time". The award went to Boyz II Men for "End of the Road". Michael's first appearance during the telecast came when he was named the Humanitarian of the Year. The award was presented by Michael's friend, Eddie Murphy:

I address these remarks to a very good friend of mine, Michael Jackson. Now, Michael, everyone knows you have broken every sales record known to man and that you have the number one and number two best selling albums of all time and the number one selling single of all time and he's the biggest selling artist ever, but tonight we're not here to talk about that, we're here to talk about your achievements as a humanitarian and your concern about the well-being of children and brothers and sisters everywhere and Mother Earth herself.

As the cheers from the crowd threatened to drown Murphy out, he cut his remarks short and said, "Hey, just show the film, huh!" A short film tribute to Michael, narrated by Eddie Murphy, outlined a few of Michael's countless efforts to help children and make the world a better place. Michael, who was on crutches, was helped to the stage from his front row seat by Bill Bray. He was dressed in black pants and a black jacket with belts across his chest, a red armband, and one shoe. After blowing kisses to the wildly cheering crowd, he apologized for his injury, and Murphy insisted he tell how it happened, "You can't just come out like that and not tell us what happened." Michael replied, "You really want to know? I was dancing and I went into a spin and I twisted my ankle very badly. But I wanted to come here to thank everyone." After poking fun at Murphy, "Eddie, I heard you have a new album out, that you're the one whose 'dangerous'", Michael continued:

Ever since I was a child, I realized I had a lot of love to share from my soul. The black tradition is a tradition of soul which is a gift of love and joy. Soul is the most precious thing you can share because you're sharing yourself and the world needs that gift now more than ever. The child with AIDS, in the ghetto, is waiting for you along with the starving people in Africa and everyone else who needs healing. Make the world more beautiful by sharing with me the wonderful feeling you get when your soul is lifted up to become pure love. I accept this award on behalf of all the children of the world who are my inspiration and my hope...

Michael's next award was for Best R&B Soul Single, Male for "Remember the Time". Michael was wheeled out from backstage in a wheelchair by Bill Bray, then he stood with the aid of a crutch to accept the award:

Thank you again, I love you all. Thank you Berry Gordy, the Sony family, Akio Morita, Mickey Schulhof, Tommy Mottola, Dave Glew, and especially Hank Caldwell. Teddy Riley, all the program directors and DJ's, you play my records, Sandy Gallin and Jim Morey and the fans.

For the presentation of the Heritage Award, Michael Jackson and Eddie Murphy traded places. This time Michael was the presenter and Eddie Murphy was the recipient. Michael has rarely, and never in more than ten years, appeared as a presenter on any award show. He was introduced by host Patti Labelle, "Please welcome the King of Pop, Rock and Soul, Mr. Michael Jackson!" Michael was wheeled out on stage in the wheelchair by Bill Bray, then stood with the aid of a crutch. As Michael began the tribute to his friend, the cheers from the crowd grew deafening and Michael had to remind them that "this is Eddie's moment":

At the young age of 31, Eddie Murphy has carved out a truly spectacular career in almost any direction he choose to go in, including stand-up comedy, television, film-acting, film-directing, television producing and music included. It would be impossible to cover all of Eddie's achievements and how brilliantly he performed in each area, but let's take a look.

After a short collection of clips from Murphy's many films, Michael introduced his friend, "Ladies and gentlemen, please welcome the recipient of the 1993 Soul Train Music Award's Heritage Award, Mr. Eddie Murphy." Eddie Murphy then said to the crowd, "Isn't it nice seeing him getting out and giving people awards and stuff?" He also thanked Michael, "for hobblin' out here and giving me this award."

Later in the broadcast Michael changed in the gold Egyptian costume he wears in the video for "Remember the Time" and he performed the song sitting in an elaborate gold chair placed in the center of the stage, with his dancers behind him. Seated, he gyrated from the waist up and belted out the song like nobody's business, even bringing himself up to stand, balancing himself on one foot a couple of times during the performance.

The final award of the evening was for Best R&B/Soul Album, Male, and it went to Michael Jackson for *Dangerous*. He was again wheeled out in the wheelchair from backstage by Bill Bray, he then stood on crutches. In accepting the award, Michael acknowledged one of the award presenters, Run DMC:

Run DMC, I think you're brilliant. I'd like to thank Don Cornelius, I love you Don, thank you. Thank you Berry Gordy, Dave Glew, and especially Hank Caldwell, Bob Jones, and last, the public, the fans. I love you all.

In mid March, Michael won a legal victory, something he would need to savor considering what lie ahead for him. Hugo Zucarelli sued Michael Jackson claiming he was never paid for Michael's use of recording technology Zucarelli invented, that was used in recording *Bad*. A judge dismissed the suit, after which Zucarelli reportedly struck one of Michael's attorney's and shoved another. He also hit an attorney from Sony. Zucarelli was booked on battery charges and released on his own recognizance.

Also in March, Michael won approval from officials in Santa Barbara County to build a twenty acre breeding ground for apes, white tigers, bears, and other animals on his ranch.

Wondering how a toy factory looked and just how toys are made, Michael asked to visit the Hasbro factory in Pawtucket, Rhode Island. He visited the factory on April 14, and checked out the production line and fun room where toys are tested. He also visited with children and signed autographs.

Following Michael's revealing interview with Oprah Winfrey and the resulting media frenzy, several members of the Jackson family appeared on the magazine show, *Day One*, in April, and talked with Michel McQueen. Joseph and Katherine, Rebbie, Jackie, Tito, Jermaine, and Randy spoke of Joe's strictness while they were growing up. They confirmed Joe was very strict and did beat them but refused to label the whippings as child abuse. The family, especially Jermaine, addressed issues regarding Michael's success. Jermaine denied he was jealous of Michael's fame and said he wrote his song condemning Michael, "Word to the Badd" out of anger that his phone calls to Michael weren't being returned. Tito stated the music, melodies, and moves come very easy to Michael, certainly easier than it comes to Tito, "Dancing like Michael Jackson is a nightmare for me."

The family also answered the charges of physical and sexual abuse being made by LaToya, with each of them denying it and stating they didn't know why she was making those statements.

The same time the *Day One* program aired, LaToya was having difficulties with the Internal Revenue Service. It was being reported that the IRS was set to auction off LaToya's share of Hayvenhurst, the family's Encino home, to pay her $511,000 tax bill due for 1988, 1989, and 1991. The bill was paid at the last minute and the auction never took place. It has been reported that the bill was picked up by brother Michael. In an earlier arrangement concerning a lawsuit involving Joe, the deed to Hayvenhurst had been turned over to LaToya. It was meant as a temporary arrangement, but then LaToya wouldn't return it. In paying her tax bill, Michael took back the deed to Hayvenhurst and saved the family's Encino home.

LaToya had bigger problems just a few days later when her husband and manager, Jack Gordon, was arrested for striking LaToya in the face, arms, and legs with a dining room chair. LaToya was treated for her injuries and released from Lenox Hill Hospital. Criminal charges of assault and weapons violations against Gordon were dropped when LaToya decided to press a civil assault case in New York's Family Court. Gordon, at the time, claimed he was defending himself against a knife attack by his wife. The couple later claimed the attack was due to mood swings Gordon suffered in reaction to radiation therapy he was receiving for treatment for cancer.

On April 15, 1993, a music video debuted on the Fox network and BET. This was not a Michael Jackson video, however, he did appear in it. Eddie Murphy's video for "Whatzupwitu" from his album, *Love's Alright*, featured Michael Jackson and the Boys Choir of Harlem. The video is a light hearted look at Eddie and Michael singing and dancing against a backdrop of clouds, birds, and flowers. The single did surprisingly poor on the charts, going only to seventy four on the R&B singles chart and never making a showing on the pop chart.

Michael next joined former President Jimmy Carter in Atlanta on May 5 for Heal Atlanta, part of Michael's Heal the World Foundation. The Immunization/Children's Health Initiative was open to children under six who live in Atlanta projects and have current immunization certificates.

The American Film Institute Salute To Elizabeth Taylor aired on May 6, 1993. The tribute, filmed nearly two months earlier, was attended by Michael Jackson, who was still on crutches due to his ankle injury. The tribute consisted of short clips of her movies with short remembrances from various friends and co-stars. Taylor sat at a table between her husband, Larry Fortensky, and her friend, Michael Jackson. Michael was not one of the speakers in the program.

He did contribute to another tribute to Elizabeth Taylor that aired as part of the Arts & Entertainment network's *Biography* series. The special, filmed in the spring, aired for the first time on September 7, 1993. Michael was interviewed for the special by A&E's Cathy Griffen who said she planned to give him a Mickey Mouse waffle maker to mark his second interview in two weeks! In the interview, Michael explained one of the things he and Elizabeth Taylor have in common, "We shared a quest in search of the next step of acceptance from an adoring public who never really knew our inner turmoil". By the time this tribute to Taylor aired, Michael was embroiled in turmoil he couldn't have possibly imagined.

2

M.J. 4 EVER

Michael picked up an honor on May 19, from the Guiness World of Records Museum, who presented him with the first ever Lifetime Achievement Award. The award was in recognition of his many world records: the best selling album in history (*Thriller*), winning the most Grammys in a single year (Eight in 1984), the biggest concert (500,000 people in four shows at London's Wembley Stadium), the biggest contract in the history of show business, (Signed with Sony in 1991), and performing before the largest ever television audience (133.4 million during his halftime performance at the 1993 Super Bowl).

The master of ceremonies for the event was Casey Kasem and the founding editor of the *Guiness Book of World Records*, Norris McWhirter, flew to Los Angeles from London especially to present the honor. Michael, dressed in black, with large mirrored sunglasses and a fedora, accepted the honor and spoke to the crowd of fans that had brought Hollywood Blvd. to a standstill, "I love you all and thank you very much for coming."

Lori Byler, president of the Michael Jackson Observer Fan Club, then presented Michael with a second award. The plague was in recognition of his work with children and its inscription read:

In deepest appreciation for all you have done for the children of the world, Because of your great love and sensitivity towards all children, they now have the chance to live a happy and normal life. Without other great humanitarians, like yourself, the lives and future of our children the world over is hopeless.

All of us wish to join hands with you, Michael, to help Heal the World and to preserve the future for all the children of the world.

We, the members of the Michael Jackson Observer Fan Club wish to offer you our support, love, loyalty and appreciation for everything you have done for our children, and for all of us.

With our deepest respect and love,
The Michael Jackson Observer Fan Club
of the United States and around the world.

Following the award presentations, Michael went inside the museum to unveil an updated lifesize likeness of himself being added to the museum's display. The figure of himself stands on top of a giant 45 rpm record in recognition of his unprecedented world records in entertainment. Also part of the display are Michael's albums, memorabilia, and video monitors playing highlights from his entire career. The wax figure later need repairs when it was damaged in the earthquake that rocked California in January.

There were two Jackson nominations for the first American Television Awards; *The Jacksons: An American Dream* was nominated for Best Mini Series, but didn't win. *Michael Jackson Talks To ... Oprah* was nominated for Best News, Information or Documentary, but it didn't win either. Michael did not attend the award presentation.

Airing on June 1, 1993 were the World Music Awards that were actually held on May 12 at the Sporting Club in Monte Carlo. The World Music Awards were established by Prince Albert of Monaco to recognize the top selling artists in major international markets and genres. This year the awards were being telecast in the U.S. for the first time. Helping to increase their stature and credibility was the presence of the King of Pop who would be attending, not to sing and dance, but to pick up three of their biggest honors.

He received his first award of the evening from the program's host, Michael Douglas:

It wasn't difficult to determine the Best Selling American Artist this year. His records have been at the top of the charts for over 24 years. He sold more records than any other individual in recording history. His televised interview was one of the most watched shows of all time and you can hear the screams anytime he even thinks of appearing on stage anywhere. In this princely principality, it may be considered inappropriate to introduce a king, but indulge me this once as I introduce this year's Best Selling American Artist, the King of Pop, Michael Jackson.

The crowd rose to its feet as Michael ascended the stairs to the stage. He was seated in the front row of the Sporting Club with a little girl, and a young boy who was dressed as Michael in a black jacket and a black fedora. Michael was dressed in black pants, a wide metallic belt, black and silver boots, and a black jacket with a red armband over a white t-shirt. He also wore a black fedora and large mirrored sunglasses.

Thanks to all my fans and friends in America for your continued support of my music. Thanks to Mickey Schulhof, Tommy Mottola, Dave Glew, and my entire Sony family, you made it happen. Thanks to Sandy Gallin and Jim Morey. I love you all. Thank you very much.

For Michael's second honor, Michael Douglas introduced a montage of video clips and concert footage of Michael Jackson. Sir John Morgan, president of the International Federation of the Phonographic Industry, next introduced Princess Stephanie of Monaco. She in turn introduced Michael:

The name of this year's Best Selling Pop Artist I'm sure will come as no surprise to anyone. He has been ruling the charts for some time now with a musical style that blends Pop, Rock, R&B, Gospel, Rap, and Motown. It is a combination that has captivated the world and garnered him with this year's World Music Award as Best Selling Pop Artist and his name is Michael Jackson.

In accepting his second award of the evening, Michael took time to recognize another Motown group who had performed on the program:

Thank you, Michael Douglas, thank you Sir John Morgan, and Princess Stephanie. Thank you so much.

*Boyz II Men, I think you're brilliant. Thanks to my fans around the world for making my album, **Dangerous** the biggest selling album of '92. You continue to make my dreams a reality. Thanks to my Sony International family which made it happen. I love you madly. Thank you.*

Prince Albert of Monaco presented the final award of the evening for World's Best Selling Artist of the Era:

...Congratulations to all the artists whose work has been recognized here tonight. Only one recording artist is receiving three World Music Awards this year. As you have recently seen the accolades are justified. He not only set standards for all artists in sales and use of recording and video media but he demonstrates how the power of celebrity can be used to positive effect in helping to ease the problems of our world. It is with great pleasure that I present him with this award which names him World's Best Selling Artist of the Era. Once again, ladies and gentlemen, the King of Pop, Mr. Michael Jackson!

Michael walked out from backstage carrying his two awards he had won earlier then collected his third honor from Prince Albert. In the middle of this acceptance remarks, he asked Prince Albert to hold one of his trophies:

Thank you, your Serene Highness. I am honored to accept this World Music Award. It means a lot to me, for I sincerely believe that thorough music... could you hold this for me? Would you mind? Sorry, it's kind of heavy.

Then he continued:

> *I believe that through music we can help heal the world. It's through such charities as the Princess Grace Foundation of Monaco that this will be accomplished. Again, thanks to my fans around the world, I love you, and you wonderful people of Monaco for these honors. Merci, merci, encore!*"

The crowd was cheering wildly, calling "Michael!, Michael!, Michael!", and a banner was held up reading, "M.J. 4 Ever".

Immediately following the World Music Awards presentation, Michael was pushed to the floor by an over zealous fan. The Italian fan was trying to get close to his idol and give him a hug. Michael said later, "He just got over excited". This incident was over as quickly as it happened. Unfortunately, the world would later hear more than they ever expected, or wanted, from the young boy who attended the award show with Michael.

An ad in the June 5, 1993 issue of *Billboard* magazine congratulated the winners at the World Music Awards. In the center of the page was the biggest winner, a photo of Michael holding his three heavy awards.

The June 12, 1993 issue of *Billboard* offered a special section devoted to Rhythm and Blues. An overview of 1983 stated, "While it's impossible to consider the music of the 80's without thinking of Michael Jackson, he actually made his first appearance on the R&B charts in the 60's." A recap of Michael's chart performance on the R&B charts throughout the year 1983 concluded, "No artist has so dominated one calendar year since."

Premiere magazine reported in June that Columbia Pictures had purchased the rights to develop a movie based on Jack and the Beanstalk with Michael Jackson in mind. Columbia however, denied any knowledge of the project.

After months of persistence by *Life* magazine's director of photography, David Friend, the first ever photos of Michael Jackson's Neverland Valley Ranch were featured in the June 1993 issue of *Life* magazine. The photographs were taken by Harry Benson. The "Michael in Wonderland" photo spread featured photos of the gorgeous, meticulously manicured, grounds of Michael's ranch, and the amusement park. There were also pictures of Michael surrounded by the children of his staff members, and several of his pets, including a first look at his twelve foot albino python, named Madonna, named so, according to Michael, "because she's blond, but *I* didn't name her that." The cover photo had Michael seated with two chimps in his lap, and surrounded by a llama, a miniature horse, and an exotic bird.

The series of photographs showed the splendor of Neverland and David Friend's accompanying text explains its owner's vision while visiting the movie theater with the hospital beds built in for young visitors too ill to sit up:

It is here, standing next to the hospital beds, that one understands the essence of Neverland to its owner, amusement is hardly the point of the place. This is actually the world Jackson would fashion were it left in his charge: safe and clean and timeless as a fable.

Unfortunately, these words and this ideal would be quickly forgotten in a couple of months.

Michael was also featured on the June cover of *Disney's Adventure* magazine with Pinocchio. In return for posing for the cover, he asked for a subscription to the magazine, and he received a Disney Adventures jacket. The issue offered "25 Things You Probably Didn't Know About Michael Jackson" that most fans probably already knew.

As usual, Michael's other activities revolved around entertaining and helping children. A rally was held at a middle school in Los Angeles on June 10, to launch a new D.A.R.E. program for the school aimed at helping to keep kids off of drugs and out of gangs. The new program, D.A.R.E. P.L.U.S. (Play and Learn Under Supervision), is supported by a number of celebrities, many of whom attended the rally. The celebrity who reportedly caused the biggest stir was the King of Pop. Michael was presented with a t-shirt, and said, "Thank you very much. I love you all. Thank you." Michael is a member of the Board of Directors of D.A.R.E. (Drug Abuse Resistance Education.)

A few days later, Michael attended the opening of the Back To The Future ride at Universal Studios in Hollywood. He snuck in a back entrance to avoid the media that was covering the opening of the ride.

Michael hosted a group of one hundred children at his ranch in June from the Challengers Boys and Girls Club in Los Angeles. The Big Brothers of Los Angeles gave Michael a rocking chair made by the woman who made them for President Kennedy and the Pope.

Another group of children visiting the ranch got a sneak peak preview of *Tom & Jerry: The Movie*. The film wasn't scheduled to begin running in theaters until

July 30, but Michael received an advance copy from Joseph Barbera.

Together For Our Children, a syndicated special, began airing in June. The special was put together to help raise funds for children's immunization. Michael lent a performance of "Jam" from London's Wembley Stadium to be included in the special.

Sotheby's held its semi-annual auction of Rock & Roll memorabilia on June 23. Michael Jackson's "Beat It" jacket was purchased by the Hard Rock Cafe for $7,762.

A self portrait of Michael Jackson was on tour throughout the summer as part of the Image Makers Rock 'n Roll Art Exposition. The exposition opened at the Boston Center for the Arts and included works by John Lennon, Yoko Ono, Ron Wood, David Bowie, Miles Davis, Donna Summer, and others.

In early July, Michael sent Mallory Cyr, an eight year old girl suffering from a rare intestinal disease, a check and a promise to call. He had responded to a letter writing campaign conducted by school children in Sabattus, Maine. Michael's note read, "I am sending you all my loving and caring, Mallory, along with the enclosed gift, which I hope will help nourish you and keep you strong."

Free Willy, a movie of a young boy's efforts to free a whale from a theme park, began airing in theaters on July 16. The soundtrack for the film, the first release on Michael's MJJ Records label, featured "Will You Be There" as the movie's theme song. Also included on the soundtrack was "Right Here" by SWV (Sisters With Voices), that included a sampling of Michael's "Human Nature". T3, made up of Taj, Taryll, and Tito Jackson Jr., contributed "Didn't Mean To Hurt You" to Uncle

Mike's first release on his record label. The *Free Willy* soundtrack album peaked at number forty seven on *Billboard's* pop album chart, and at number forty nine on the R&B album chart.

The lyrics to "Will You Be There", Michael's contribution to the soundtrack, would become more poignant in just a few weeks:

> *In our darkest hour*
> *In my deepest despair*
> *Will you still care?*
> *Will you be there?*

The video for Michael's latest single combines footage of whales swimming and frolicking freely in the ocean with Michael's performance of the song in concert. Smooth and graceful choreography showcase his performance, complete with an angel descending and wrapping her wings around him.

Sisters With Voices enjoyed a huge hit with "Right Here/Human Nature". The song's accompanying video incorporated footage from *Free Willy* and of Michael's performance of "Human Nature" from the Dangerous tour.

Michael's record label, which was part of his 1991 mega deal with Sony, was originally reported to be named Nation Records, in recognition of Janet's massive success with *Janet Jackson's Rhythm Nation 1814*. Michael had hoped his sister would be one of the artists to sign with his new label. Janet, who has long fought to succeed on her own without benefit of her big brother, thought better of the idea. She ended up signing a new recording contract with Virgin Records that made her the artist with the biggest recording contract in history, at least for a few days. Within days of Janet's announcement, it was announced that Michael Jackson had re-signed with Sony. His new deal with Sony was reported to have billion dollar potential.

In July, 1993, Michael Jackson was announced as the recipient of the 1994 Scopus Award to be presented at the Beverly Hilton Hotel on January 29, 1994. The award, from the American Friends of Hebrew University, was in recognition of his international humanitarian efforts .

Jack the Rapper Awards, handed out in August in Atlanta, honored Motown founder Berry Gordy with the Original 13 Award for his legendary work in the music industry. The Our Children, Our Hope of Tomorrow Award, which was named after Michael Jackson, was awarded to, well, Michael Jackson. In a videotaped message Michael said, "I am honored and humbled."

A $50 million lawsuit was filed against Michael Jackson in August to get access to Beatle songs for rappers to perform. Jay Bildstein, of 57 Entertainment, claimed Michael Jackson gave permission for rappers to do versions of "Help" and "Lady Madonna" but later reneged on the deal after checking with Paul McCartney and Yoko Ono. Michael's attorney said no agreement was reached where license was required. Paul McCartney, Yoko Ono, and Michael Jackson were all ordered to give court depositions in the case. But this matter would be the least of Michael's legal problems.

As the opening dates of the Asian leg of the Dangerous tour grew nearer, the dates kept changing. Shows were scheduled, then canceled, with dates and cities being changed frequently. U.S. Embassy officials in Seoul, Korea, tried to change a decision made by the

Ministry of Culture denying Michael Jackson an opportunity to have a concert there. The South Korean officials were concerned about protecting any threats to their traditional confucian values such as loud pop music and suggestive choreography.

Originally, the tour was to begin in Hong Kong with shows on August 15th and 16th. Those dates, to be held at Shatin Racecourse, were canceled and could not be rescheduled because it would conflict with the start of the racing season. Finally, August 24, 1993 was announced as the opening show of the Dangerous tour in Bangkok, Thailand.

As usual, this was to be no small production. Michael would be performing on a stage wider than any stage in America. The widest stage in America is at New York's Radio City Music Hall, which is 190 feet across. Michael's stage measured 270 feet across and took four days to set up and three days to take down. The equipment necessary to stage the show and create the special effects included 168 speakers, 9 video screens, and nearly 1,000 lights which were specially designed to be effective in darkness or daylight. All of this was powered by four generators which would be sufficient to light up a small town.

However the excitement of the opening of the tour would be buried by shock and disbelief at reports that Michael Jackson was under criminal investigation by the Los Angeles Police Department, creating the biggest scandal in Michael Jackson's career and quite possibly, all of show business. The investigation, which actually began on August 17, 1993, was brought on by the thirteen year old boy who, with his mother and step sister, had accompanied Michael to Monte Carlo in May for the World Music Awards. The boy had made claims of child molestation against Michael Jackson.

3

AUGUST 17, 1993

T he boy's claims were unsubstantiated, however, his accusations did prompt the Los Angeles police department to open an investigation on August 17, 1993, and to serve search warrants on Michael's Neverland Valley Ranch and his condo in Century City, on August 21 and 22. Michael was not home at the time of the search, having already flown to Bangkok for the kick off of the tour. A locksmith accompanied the police officers during the search to help them gain entry to rooms which were locked and to which the household staff had no keys. Jackson's camp cooperated with the search. Several boxes of photographs and videotapes were removed from the premises. These were erroneously referred to by some members of the media as evidence, when in fact the photos and videos showed nothing out of the ordinary, and didn't incriminate Michael at all. A source from the police department told *The Los Angeles Times*, "There's no medical evidence, no taped evidence ... The search warrant didn't result in anything that would support a criminal filing."

Immediately questions arouse as to how the LAPD was able to obtain the search warrants for Michael's homes based solely on the unsubstantiated claims of one boy. In requesting a search warrant, police are required to prove they have probable cause that a crime has been committed. In this case, they had no such thing.

With no evidence to be found, investigators from the police department's Sexually Exploited Child Unit, who were leading the investigation, then concentrated on interviewing other youngsters who are friends of Michael's in an attempt to find someone who would corroborate the boy's story. The thirteen year old boy gave authorities the names of four other boys he said he believed were also molested by Michael Jackson. These four, all said to be well known friends of Michael's, included child actor Macaulay Culkin. Culkin was questioned by police and he stated there was never any inappropriate behavior by Michael Jackson. The other boys questioned by police also said there was never any improper conduct by Michael.

In reporting on the story, *Hard Copy* correspondent Diane Dimond reported, "And one more shocker, *Hard Copy* had obtained new documents in the criminal investigation of Michael Jackson and they are chilling, they contain the name of child movie actor Macaulay Culkin." Delicately tip toeing around the facts, this teaser certainly suggests Culkin was another "victim" of abuse by Michael Jackson. What was conveniently ignored is that Culkin told police there was never any improper conduct by Michael.

Michael's investigator, Anthony Pellicano, explained at a press conference on August 24, that the allegations were the result of a plot by the boy's father to extort $20 million from Michael Jackson, "A demand for $20 million was made and presented. It was flatly and consistently refused. The refusals have in our opinion caused what has transpired in the last few days ... When we would not pay, a phone call was made to Child and Family Services, which started this investigation." When Michael refused to be hustled, the allegations were taken public, carefully orchestrated no doubt, to coincide with the opening of the Dangerous tour.

When Michael's newly hired criminal lawyer, Howard Weitzman, was asked at this press conference why the extortion attempt wasn't reported to the police, he replied, "It was our hope that this would all go away. We tried to keep it as much in-house as we could." Weitzman then read a statement to the press from Michael:

My representatives have continuously kept me aware of what is taking place in California. I appreciate the remarks of Chief Willie Williams and our Los Angeles police department. I am confident the department will conduct a fair and thorough investigation and its results will demonstrate that there was no wrongdoing on my part. I intend to continue with my world tour, and look forward to seeing all of you in the scheduled cities. I am grateful for the overwhelming support of my fans throughout the world. I love you all. Thank you. Michael.

A separate investigation was then begun by the Los Angeles police department to investigate the boy's father and the more plausible extortion claims. This of course wasn't as juicy as the investigation against Michael, so it received relatively little attention in the media. But it too would last for several months.

Coverage of the abuse allegations was top story news on virtually all morning and evening news casts, all entertainment news programs, and front page news on newspapers for days. Scandal hungry tabloid TV shows wouldn't let go of the story for months. With a few exceptions, the identities of the boy and his father were concealed by the media. Photos of Michael with the young boy had the boy's face blocked out or blurred, and their names in documents were blackened out. God forbid if their lives would become disrupted due to the media's unrelenting and intense scrutiny into their personal lives prompted merely by accusations of extortion that were as of yet, unproven. Their names will not be hidden here as they are really no longer a very big secret, having been published by a few sources early on in the coverage of the story. The names were even easily readable through the black marker scandal shows used on court documents to conceal them.

Meanwhile, the kick off of the Dangerous tour in Bangkok went on as planned. Michael dazzled and thrilled the soldout crowd starting with "Jam" and not letting up for two hours with his unsurpassed talent and showmanship. The crowd was unconcerned with the allegations being made against Michael and the media eruption, continuing to cheer him and holding up banners supporting him.

Soon after the press conference held on August 24 by Pellicano and Weitzman, another investigator entered the picture. Ernie Rizzo, an investigator from Chicago who had lost his license for illegal wire tapping, came forward and said he was representing the boy's father. This was denied by the father's attorney, Richard Hirsch, who said Rizzo was not being retained by anyone connected to the case. While Rizzo would later turn up on a talk show or two, he actually had little if anything to do with the case and is really just a long time adversary of Anthony Pellicano.

Experts in various areas of the entertainment field, not necessarily directly concerned with Michael Jackson, stated in numerous interviews that someone of Michael Jackson's status is an easy target for extortion. Michael Jackson was seen as an especially easy target for child abuse allegations because his deep affection for children is so well known and he spends so much time with children. Michael Jackson biographer J. Randy Taraborrelli, surprisingly, consistently supported Michael and the claims of extortion, "I've seen so many extortion attempts against the Jackson camp and they never turnout to be worth anything." Taraborrelli told *Time* magazine that in researching his book on Jackson, "every damn butler, housekeeper, chauffeur and chef wanted $100,000 for their insights into his private life. I've written about Diana Ross, Cher, Carol Burnett, and Roseanne Arnold, but I never had that experience with any of my other books. And that was just me, a biographer. You can imagine what it's like for him with his millions."

As the story broke on virtually every possible outlet, Commander David Gascon of the Los Angeles Police Department would only confirm that a criminal investigation was indeed being conducted involving Michael Jackson but refused to discuss any details because, "we do not want to feed any wild speculation on this matter". That was certainly a wise move, otherwise the media might get completely out of control and start airing reports based solely on rumors and innuendo. Before you know it tabloid magazines and scandal shows like, oh *Hard Copy,* might offer people a lot of money for anything negative to report on Michael Jackson. The story would then continue to grow with more and more people suddenly remembering things they saw several months, or even several years, earlier that somehow now seemed to be relevant to this story, making the "Michael Jackson Scandal" the dominating story for these magazines and television shows for months. No, that's too ridiculous, that would never happen.

Actually the Los Angeles Police Department would turn out to be one of the biggest leaks of information in the whole investigation. Within just a few days, two tabloid TV shows had copies of confidential documents in the case from the Los Angeles County Department of Children's Services. Each show paid over $10,000 for the copies of the documents. And this certainly wouldn't be the end of the tabloid magazines' and TV shows' efforts to buy any information in the Michael Jackson case. As long as it was something negative, they were interested. And they would soon be bombarded with offers. The more money that was being offered, the more juicy the stories became.

It was learned that the boy's father, let's call him Evan Chandler, was a Beverly Hills dentist who wished he was a screenwriter. He had recently had one screenplay made into a movie that was based on an idea of his son's. The boy's parents, married in 1974, divorced in 1985 and were both now remarried and were involved in a bitter custody battle for the boy. It was also learned that Chandler was delinquent in his child support payments by $68,400.

Michael first met the young boy one day in May, 1992, when his car stalled near a Rent-A-Wreck car rental company. Michael went to the car rental company to rent a car while his was repaired. The owner of the company quickly phoned his family and told them to come to the office to meet Michael Jackson. Michael and the owner's stepson, Jordy, quickly became friends with Michael calling the boy frequently.

Michael then began inviting Jordy, his stepsister and his mother to visits to Neverland. They would spend weekends at Neverland, or take trips together to Las Vegas and Florida. In May of 1993, they accompanied Michael to Monte Carlo for the World Music Awards. These weekend trips began to interfere with the boy's scheduled visits with his father. When Jordy preferred to go to Neverland for the weekend instead of spending time with his father, Chandler became furious. As part of the ongoing custody battle, Chandler filed a court document requesting the mother "not to allow the minor child to have any contact or communication with a third party adult male known as Michael Jackson." This raises an important question. If Michael Jackson were actually molesting the boy, why would he ever choose to visit Neverland over a scheduled visit with his father? He certainly was old enough to decide for himself whether he would spend the weekend with his father, or with Michael Jackson.

The boy's mother, who was with the boy on his visits with Michael, first learned of the allegations from police, not from her son or his father, and was completely shocked. She said she had no indication anything untoward was going on.

Numerous experts in the field of child abuse, and experts in family law, pointed out that bitter custody battles such as this one were often used to levy false child abuse allegations to gain the advantage in the case. In this case, the father wanted to regain custody of his son who had been missing scheduled weekend visits with his father so he could spend time at Neverland. One expert pointed out that "there are therapists who interview children in ways that are leading, suggestive and coercive; they are the validators of sexual abuse charges." A lawyer added, "You're looking at a thirteen year old child in the middle of a bitter custody fight. These children are the least reliable witnesses of all, because they're being torn between pleasing two parents. They're trying to protect themselves. Often children side with one parent or the other and say what that parent wants to hear."

To gain the advantage in the custody fight is only one possible motive the father may have had in filing a false claim of child abuse. The most obvious in this particular case is money. That will be explored in detail here. One other possible motive is jealousy. The father was furious when his boy choose to visit Michael Jackson at Neverland over his scheduled visit with his father. These possible motives along with big holes in some of the statements made by the boy, his father and others, raises series questions about their credibility.

According to the boy's testimony in court documents, his relationship with Michael heated up while they were in Monaco, and ended in July. Why then did the boy seem very comfortable and happy at Neverland with Michael when Ryan White's mother, Jeanne, met him there in July? Mrs. White-Ginder stated the boy was not uncomfortable, "I saw nothing out of the ordinary. Believe me, that young man was not afraid of Michael at all. He behaved just like a normal thirteen year old." And why, did it take a court petition filed in August, to prevent the boy from having any contact with Michael Jackson? It is certainly understandable that if someone is abused, they would feel frightened and embarrassed, and not tell anyone of the situation. Victims of child abuse have gone from childhood to adulthood without ever revealing the abuse they were subjected to. But what doesn't fit in this case is that the boy repeatedly *chose* to visit Neverland over scheduled visits with his father. Why, if he was actually being molested on these visits, would he put himself in those situations unnecessarily? He was thirteen years old, not an infant, he certainly had a choice in whether he wanted to visit Michael Jackson or stay with his father for the weekend.

It was reported that Chandler asked Michael Jackson to set him up with film projects in the amount of $5 million per year for four years, for a total of $20 million, or he would go public with child abuse allegations. When his offer was refused by Michael Jackson, the father became furious.

On July 12, 1993, a meeting was held with the boy's mother, stepfather, Michael's attorney, Bert Fields and investigator Anthony Pellicano. There the stepfather played tapes of phone conversations between himself and Chandler in which Chandler accuses Michael of molesting his son. Pellicano then drove to Michael's Century City condo where Jordy and his stepsister were staying. He talked with Jordy for forty five minutes, asking very direct, specific questions about his relationship with Michael Jackson. Pellicano asked Jordy if Michael had ever touched him, if Michael had ever masturbated in front of him, or if Michael ever masturbated him. The boy answered "no" to each and every question. Pellicano asked if he had ever seen Michael's body, and the boy said no, but he did lift his shirt once to show him the blotches on his skin. Pellicano then asked Michael the same questions, he also said nothing happened. Jordy then complained that his father always wanted him to sit in the house and write screenplays, and that his father just wanted money.

The boy was now staying with his father. Chandler had demanded that the boy be allowed to visit him for the week of July 11. At the end of the week, he refused to return the boy to his mother. A meeting was held on August 4 with Michael Jackson, Anthony Pellicano, Chandler and Jordy. According to Pellicano, when the father accused Michael of molesting his son, Michael cried and said, "I would never do that to your little boy." Jordy reportedly looked up at Michael with a startled expression of disbelief at what his father was accusing Michael Jackson.

Meanwhile, the custody battle continued. Michael Freeman, the attorney representing the boy's mother, filed a petition in court demanding the return of her son. The judge ordered Chandler to return the boy to his mother by 6:00 p.m. on August 17 and he refused Chandler's request for Jordy to have no further contact with Michael Jackson.

That very morning, Chandler took his son to a therapist, where he preceded to describe his alleged relationship, in detail, with Michael Jackson. The therapist then reported the allegations to Child and Family Services, as is required by California law. That, not a complaint by the father, instigated the criminal investigation against Michael Jackson. It is doubtful the father realized the therapist would be obligated to make the report to the police, he hadn't yet finished negotiating his movie 1eal.

In response to the report made by the therapist, custody of the boy was then immediately given to Los Angeles County. The report of abuse by Child and Family Services took precedence over the earlier ruling demanding the return of the boy to his mother. He was allowed to stay at his father's house, but with many restrictions.

Anthony Pellicano produced audio tapes of phone conversations between Chandler and the boy's step father, which Pellicano said proved the extortion plot. The phone conversations, taped by the boy's stepfather, had Chandler threatening to destroy Michael Jackson, "It's going to be a massacre if I don't get what I want ... This man is gong to be humiliated beyond belief. He will not believe what is going to happen to him - beyond his worst nightmares ... He won't sell one more record. If I go through with this, I win big time. I will get everything I want. They will be destroyed forever." Whether or not these tapes actually prove an extortion attempt on behalf of the father, there were certainly many indications that he was very interested in profiting from the whole thing. Instead of making any report to the police for what supposedly happened to his son, he arranged a meeting with Michael and his attorneys to discuss movie deals. The father initially asked for funding for four movies, at $5 million each, a total of $20 million. This was refused by the Jackson camp and a counter offer of $350,000 for one movie was made. After considering it, Chandler refused.

Throughout the whole ugly media massacre, there had been no indication from the boy or his father that they wanted Michael Jackson criminally punished for his supposed crime. When a parent truly believes their child has been mistreated, they first and foremost want the perpetrator punished, either by death or a lengthy prison sentence. They don't simply hope the person responsible is embarrassed and loses their job, even if they are the biggest pop star in the world.

A phone conversation on August 17, secretly taped by Pellicano, has Pellicano asking Chandler's attorney Barry Rothman, why the counter offer of $350,000 was turned down. Pellicano, well known for taping conversations, taped this one hoping to get confirmation on tape that the dentist only wanted money. Rothman is obviously aware he could be recorded and refuses to discuss the father's demand for the $20 million deal saying only, "We're past that point" and telling Pellicano, "you (Pellicano) sat across the table from him (Chandler) and said, 'It's not going to be that figure'...", refusing to even mention the $20 million amount. According to Pellicano, Rothman refused the one picture deal for $350,000 because Pellicano had earlier offered a three picture deal for $350,000 each and was now backing down. According to Pellicano, the one picture deal was refused because it wasn't enough for Chandler to shut down his dental practice and focus on writing screenplays full time. Pellicano told Rothman, "I'm willing to give him $350,000 to develop a project." Rothman answered, "Out of your pocket, huh?" "No", Pellicano replied, "Out of Michael's pocket, $350,000 to develop a project and that is the absolute going rate in town. You know that." "I'm not contesting the going rate," Rothman answered. Pellicano continued, "So, he's got Michael Jackson backing him up on a project which is gonna get everybody's attention and make everyone think this is a great thing. And he's gonna walk in the door with this." Rothman, still trying to get this deal for three projects added, "Instead of trying to convince me to do it on a one project basis, why don't you convince your people to do it on a three project basis." Clearly this conversation is centered on money and movie deals, not molestation.

Michael's concert scheduled for Wednesday, August 25, was postponed until the next day as Michael was suffering from acute dehydration and was under a doctor's care. He was receiving liquids intravenously. The dehydration was said to be brought on by the heat and high humidity in Bangkok, and not from the stress of the investigation.

Elizabeth Taylor, set to begin an eight city tour to promote her new line of fragrances, canceled her scheduled appearance at Sotheby's in New York to fly to Singapore to be at Michael's side. After the concerts in Bangkok, the Dangerous tour would move on to Singapore. Mike Watkiss, a story hustler for *A Current Affair*, tagged along on Taylor's flight with a cameraman. She granted him a brief interview in which she fervently defended Michael:

I believe totally that Michael will be vindicated. I believe in Michael's integrity, his love and respect of children. I know it will all come out alright. He's here all alone. He's going through a terrible time and I just wanted to be with him.

Ignoring such supportive remarks by the likes of Elizabeth Taylor and Alfonso Ribeiro, *A Current Affair's* title of their Michael Jackson story this night was "Scandal of the Decade". They, along with their chief competitor, *Hard Copy,* would continue to have outrageous stories with equally outrageous and misleading headlines and titles for several months.

Tour sponsor Pepsi's chief competitor immediately began running ads in newspapers, and put up billboards in Bangkok reading, "Dehydrated? There's Always Coke". The ads were immediately pulled after several complaints were received that they were in poor taste.

USA Today, in an article on the allegations being made against Michael, carried a quote from an unlikely, and it turns out fickle, ally Jack Gordon, who said that the allegations were "totally not true." "He really loves children. He would never harm a child."

On Thursday it was being reported in the news that the investigation had widened to include four more boys, some programs went so far as to say in their "teasers" that there were more allegations being made against Michael by additional boys. Headlines reading, "Pop star inquiry expands to 4 boys" also misled readers into believing there were more allegations being made against Michael Jackson by additional boys. This was absolutely not the case. The police had *interviewed* four more boys, all friends of Michael's, about their relationship with him in an attempt to find corroboration for the thirteen year old's story. The police found nothing to support the abuse claims. All of the boys interviewed told police their relationship with Michael was purely brotherly, that there was no inappropriate behavior on Michael's part whatsoever.

One of the young boys interviewed was eleven year old Brett Barnes, from Melbourne, Australia. Brett was a pen pal of Michael's who Michael had flown to California, with his mother and sister. Brett and his family were at Michael's ranch when the police conducted their search. The boy vehemently defended his friend telling a Los Angeles TV station, KNBC, "He's like a best friend, except he's big". He admitted that he had shared a bed with Michael, that both were fully dressed and on opposite sides of a big bed, "He slept on one side and I slept on the other. It was a big bed." He stated further that there was no inappropriate behavior. He said Michael was affectionate, but "like a big brother". Barnes added that he did know the boy making the allegations against Michael and that he had never mentioned anything unusual happening with Michael and Barnes never saw any improper behavior.

Wade Robson, a ten year old friend of Michael's, also said he had shared a bed with Michael but they were both wearing pajamas and they "just went to sleep." He stated further that, "Michael Jackson would never do anything like this." Joy Robson, Wade's mother, was not concerned with her son's relationship with Michael Jackson, "There's nothing unusual there at all. They're good friends. They're buddies."

Finding no support for the allegations, the police then questioned these children's friends to see if anything had been shared with them about Michael's behavior. They found nothing. Again.

These admissions that Michael had shared a bed with these young boys disturbed many in the media and the public, who considered it strange behavior for a thirty five year old man. What they fail to consider is when Michael Jackson is with children, he is not an adult simply enjoying watching the kids have fun. He is right there with them, having as much, or more, fun than the kids. He adores children and he enjoys the same activities kids do, playing video games, visiting amusement parks, computer games, and having slumber parties. Michael Jackson is different from "normal" thirty five year old men. While he is very shy and self conscious off stage, on stage he becomes the most electrifying and magical performer in the world. If you put him in a boardroom, he becomes a skilled negotiator. He has been since the age of nineteen when he convinced the executives at Epic Records to allow himself and his brothers to write and produce an entire album. The result, *Destiny*, went platinum. Since then he has continually played a key role in winning the biggest contracts in entertainment and endorsements, and he has built a formidable catalog of music publishing copyrights. When Michael Jackson is surrounded by children, he becomes one of them, playing games, laughing, and playing practical jokes. So, while he is certainly not like other thirty five year old men, that does not make him a weirdo, let alone a criminal.

In a rare show of unity, the Jackson family issued a statement to the press expressing their support of Michael:

We wish to state our collective, unequivocally belief that Michael has been made the victim of a cruel and obvious attempt to take advantage of his fame and success. We know, as does the whole world, that he has dedicated his life to providing happiness for young people everywhere. His compassion for the problems of all people is legendary. Accordingly, we are confident that his dignity and humanity will prevail this most difficult time. Our entire family stands firmly at this side.

The statement was signed by Michael's parents and all of his brothers and sisters, ten Jacksons in all, which would seem to have to include LaToya.

The outpouring of support for Michael was truly overwhelming. Many went public with vehement support of Michael. People who have worked with Michael for many years made public statements of their knowledge that Michael is incapable of ever hurting a child. Jerry Kramer, who worked with Michael on *The Making of Michael Jackson's Thriller*, and *Moonwalker*, told the *Today Show* he didn't believe this was something Michael Jackson would do. He said further that he has only ever seen very normal behavior with Michael Jackson and children. Entertainment lawyer Sheldon Platt, who is Whitney Houston's attorney, explained that entertainers are perfect targets for extortion. He also expressed concern that when allegations are first made public they are treated as big, front page news. When they are later retracted or found to be false, it is treated by the media as no big deal and is buried in the middle of the newspaper.

Alfonso Ribeiro, who first met Michael when he was twelve, also expressed his support for Michael. He now stars in the Quincy Jones produced series *The Fresh Prince of Bel Air* as Carlton Banks. Mothers of young children who have spent time with Michael, including Ryan White's mother Jeanne, spoke out that they implicitly trusted Michael with their children. Michael Jackson biographers J. Randy Taraborrelli and Lisa Campbell each appeared on news programs and each stated their beliefs, through studying Michael's life for several years, that he wasn't capable of committing the acts of which he was accused. Taraborrelli said in researching Jackson's life he found that "there have been many, many accusations made against Michael Jackson and none of them *ever* panned out, never found one instance that came to be even remotely true."

Michael's dearest friend, Elizabeth Taylor, told *Newsweek* magazine that "I believe 100 percent in Michael's integrity. He'd rather cut his own wrist than harm a child. He worships children." Within a few days of the allegations being made public, she, with her husband Larry Fortensky, boarded a twenty hour flight to Singapore to be with Michael and lend him all of her support.

Michael's second concert in Bangkok had to be rescheduled for the second time when he was still suffering from dehydration. He released an audio tape which was played for the press apologizing to his fans:

To all my fans in Bangkok, Thailand, I am sorry for not performing yesterday as I am really sick and still under medical treatment. I have been instructed by my doctor not to perform before Friday, August 27, 1993. I promise all my fans to perform at the National Stadium in Bangkok on August 27. I will see you all on Friday. I love you all. Goodbye.

The second concert in Bangkok did go on Friday. The crowd of 70,000 fans chanted, "Michael, Michael" and held banners reading, "We Love You". *Entertainment Tonight* reported on the show's tremendous response saying, "the show goes on in a big way."

The Dangerous tour's sponsor, Pepsi International, was also in support of Michael. Their sponsorship of the tour continued, and they continued to air two Pepsi commercials in Asia featuring Michael Jackson. Pepsi spokesmen initially stated they supported Michael one hundred percent, this was later downgraded to a more wait and see attitude, but they maintained there was no proof of any wrongdoing on behalf of Michael Jackson and unless the investigation took a sudden downturn, they would continue to support him. It later turned out they needed no such proof, but for now they still sponsored the Dangerous tour and said publicly that they supported Michael Jackson.

Advertising executives had other ideas. They repeatedly told the press that Michael Jackson's future as a product endorser was certainly over, citing recent examples of celebrities being dropped from advertising campaigns due to scandal being attached to them. Two very important facts these experts consistently overlooked however was that the particular circumstances involved in all of these other cases were proven to be true. There were only *allegations* being made against Michael Jackson, there was no proof of any wrongdoing on his part, and no charges were filed against him. Also, the allegations were overwhelmingly seen by the buying public as an obvious attempt to extort money from the most famous and successful person in the world. Michael Jackson stood an excellent chance, despite the media's distorted and slanted coverage, to maintain his unmatched level of respect, admiration, and integrity.

Michael Jackson's future as a product endorser was the subject of *Nightline* shortly after the allegations were made public. Ted Koppel's guests were Jay Coleman, who had help set up the Pepsi deals with Michael Jackson, columnist Liz Smith, and advertising executive Jerry della Femina. Koppel pointed out that "the most fair thing would be to ignore the unsubstantiated allegations until former charges are filed. But, it doesn't work that way when someone of this stature is accused." Della Femina was convinced Michael was washed up as an endorser. Liz Smith maintained that Michael was a perfect target for this type of allegation. Jay Coleman felt differently than della Femina stating that Michael Jackson's ads for Pepsi helped make their ads stand out.

One project Michael did drop out of was that of providing a song for the upcoming movie, *Addams Family Values*. Michael was said to be involved with writing and recording a song for the film's soundtrack, and perhaps working with horror writer Stephen King for the song's video. Some reports stated Michael said he would not be able to finish the song by the release date of the movie, which was due in theaters in November. Other reports said the project was scrapped due to legal difficulties. In any event, the song was not part of the movie's soundtrack, and in a real show of sensitivity, the makers of the film turned Michael Jackson into a gag in the movie.

Perhaps the most fervent support for Michael Jackson came from his millions of fans across the globe. His accusers assumed the public allegations would destroy the King of Pop but they grossly underestimated his legions of fans, for Michael Jackson's appeal goes far beyond his soulful voice and magic feet. He represents a level of dignity, decency, and integrity that won't crumble because of some completely unfounded accusations. He has been a role model for all, but especially young people. He more than entertains, he is an inspiration to all of his fans, young and old, and they love him.

Fans interviewed for television news programs consistently said they didn't believe the allegations against Michael were true, that the accusations were a blackmailing attempt. Phone-in polls conducted by *A Current Affair* showed that 82.9% of callers did not believe the allegations. A poll of teenagers conducted by *USA Today* showed that only 39% of those polled said they were fans of Jackson's, that they admired him, but almost three-fourths of those polled said they did not believe the allegations. Eighty seven percent of black teens polled did not believe Michael Jackson was guilty of any wrongdoing. Sixty six percent of younger children, ages thirteen to fifteen, also believed Michael was innocent. A poll conducted by *Entertainment Weekly* magazine showed only 12% of those polled believed the allegations. Radio stations reported that Michael Jackson's fans were jamming the phone lines in support of him. Record sales were reported to be increased since the allegations become public. His thousands of fans jamming into stadiums in Bangkok and later Singapore and Taiwan certainly didn't seem to believe any of the allegations. Fans surrounded his hotel, sang "Heal the World", and cheered wildly when Michael would wave to them from the window.

The next set of concerts were in Singapore at the National Stadium. The first of the two shows was on August 29, 1993, Michael's thirty fifth birthday. Fans fought monsoon rains and traffic jams to attend the show. Many held banners reading, "We Love You" and "Happy Birthday" as they chanted, "We Love Michael!" During the third song of the set, the band began playing "Happy Birthday" and the capacity crowd of 47,000 sang along. Michael paced the stage, smiling, and seemed genuinely touched by the sentiment.

The second show in Singapore, on Monday, was postponed shortly before Michael was to go on stage, disappointing the capacity crowd. Michael had become ill. He had fainted backstage, was complaining of dizziness, and he was vomiting. The show was rescheduled for Wednesday. The next day Michael was given several tests, including an MRI scan, and was declared by his doctor to be fit and ready to perform on Wednesday. Michael had suffered from a severe migraine headache. To apologize to his fans in Singapore, he released a second audio taped message that was played for the press by MJJ Productions' Vice President, Bob Jones:

I was suddenly taken ill last night and I am sorry for the cancellation of my performance and I apologize for any inconvenience it might have caused my fans in Singapore. I look forward to seeing you at the stadium tomorrow. Thank you for your continued support and understanding. I love you all. Thank you.

A Current Affair's Mike Watkiss reported on the cancellation of the performance, then concluded that this was "putting the entire tour in jeopardy." How postponing one show endangers an entire tour schedule wasn't explained. Actually Michael's health was improved later and he did give his scheduled performance. It didn't hamper the rest of the tour at all. The allegations against him weren't a big enough story to report, scandal shows would continue attempt to manipulate and distort facts to embellish the story. Actually the tour's promoter, Marcel Avram, would later tell *A Current Affair*, that because of the overwhelming success of the tour, there were plans to extend it.

While in Singapore, Michael was honored with a special orchid bearing his name. The orchid accolade is usually awarded only to visiting royalty and dignitaries.

It was presented to Michael by Sony Music Entertainment Singapore managing director Terence Phung, marketing manager Ian Ng and international A&R manager Joseph Loo.

Before leaving Singapore, Michael visited the Singapore Zoo with Elizabeth Taylor and a large entourage. Plans for the zoo to close for Michael's visit could not be arranged as the zoo did not want to turn away other visitors, but they did compromise, trucking six orangutans to Michael's hotel. Michael did eventually visit the zoo, arriving right at closing time. The zoo was so excited about having Michael visit, they brought in additional animals from around the area just for his visit.

On Monday, August 30, the Jackson family held a press conference, one that had been planned well before the allegations against Michael were made. Joseph, Katherine, Rebbie, Tito, and Jermaine met with reporters to announce their plans for the *Jackson Family Honors*, a reunion special and award show to be held in December, and to air on television in January. They did however address the allegations surrounding Michael. Jermaine read a statement that the entire Jackson family supported Michael. Katherine also told reporters:

First of all, I'd like to let the world know that I'm behind my son. I don't believe any of the stuff that's being written about him, because I raised him and I know that's just a statement people are making. I love him. I've talked with him several times since this had come out and I plan to go and visit him and he knows when I'm coming.

This same day, police officers served a third search warrant in their investigation. This one for

Michael's hotel room at the Mirage Hotel in Las Vegas. After a thirty minute search, they left empty handed. They said they needed to verify a description of the room given to them by the boy. The need for this search is unclear; that the boy knew the color of the bedspread in the room hardly supports his allegations. It wasn't a secret that Michael had treated the boy, along with his mother and stepsister, to trips to Las Vegas.

The day following the Jackson Family press conference, Jermaine and Tito were scheduled to appear on the *Today Show*. After reaching the studio, a film crew from a local Los Angeles station showed up to ask questions about Michael. Jermaine and Tito walked out. They did keep a scheduled appearance on *Good Morning America* where they reluctantly answered questions concerning Michael, but were more eager to promote the *Jackson Family Honors* special.

Gloria Allred, an attorney hired on August 31 to represent the boy, held a press conference on September 2 declaring that, "my client wants to have his day in court." Within a few days of her assertion about her client that, "he is ready, he is willing, he is able to testify", she withdrew from the case and refused to disclose why. Michael Freeman, the attorney representing the boy's mother, also withdrew from the case. Larry Feldman was now representing the boy. It seemed as though the boy may not have been so willing to testify after all.

That same morning, LaToya was a guest on the *Today* show where she did a very weak job of defending her brother. While she said the public had been unfair to her brother and that "I stand by him one thousand percent...If you think about it, he has been convicted before a trial", she then, within minutes, said that she herself didn't know if the allegations were true or not and that she was not a judge, and could not make such a determination. From now on keeping track of which side of the fence LaToya was on would cause anyone to have a migraine. Her comments would sway from one extreme to the other.

A few weeks later LaToya appeared on *Maury Povich* where she complained that her brother was being convicted by the public when he had not been charged with anything. She noted she saw nothing unusual about Michael being with kids and said, "I love him and I'm with him no matter what." She stated further that she would believe the allegations when it came from Michael's mouth. It of course turned out that it didn't take this much to make her believe, or at least say she believes, the allegations, only the prospect of appearing on more and more talk shows.

LaToya admitted to Maury Povich she had been invited to attend the upcoming *Jackson Family Honors* reunion special, but she refused. Later, she would deny ever being invited to the event.

Immediately after Gloria Allred was replaced, the boy's new lawyer, Larry Feldman, filed a civil suit in Los Angeles Superior Court accusing Michael Jackson of battery, infliction of emotional distress and fraud. The suit asked for unspecified monetary damages. This action certainly seemed suspect. Following an emotional statement by their attorney that the boy was ready to go to court, that attorney is fired and replaced, with a civil suit being filed immediately. Some attorneys, not connected with this case, speculated that the filing of the civil case would kill the criminal case once the jury became aware that the plaintiffs are only interested in money. It would take much more than this however for the police investigators to give up on their investigation. Despite having no physical evidence and no corroboration for the boys allegations, the criminal investigation would continue for several months. They would consistently state deadlines by which time they expected to have a decision on whether or not to charge Michael Jackson, they would all come and go with no such decision. In mid September, the Los Angeles District Attorney's office said they expected to decide on the matter by mid October. Los Angeles District Attorney Gil Garcetti described it as a no win situation. If he files charges, people will be unhappy, if he decides there's insufficient evidence to justify filing charges, other people will be unhappy. It seemed rather than admit his investigation yielded no evidence of wrongdoing, he would decide not to decide, continuing to pour taxpayers money into an investigation and avoid the risk of making anybody unhappy and hurting their feelings.

Michael obviously could not attend the MTV Music Video Awards held on September 2, but he was in the thoughts of many the artists who did attend. There was said to be a sense of sadness in the air for one of their own that night. Attendees Cindy Crawford, Sinead O'Connor, Sharon Stone and many others all pledged their support for Michael to reporters. The only nomination any of Michael's videos received was for Barry Lather's work on the choreography for "Jam". The Best Choreography award went to Envogue's video for "Free Your Mind".

Janet performed live on the award telecast. It was reported that she then planned to join Michael on his tour in a show of support for her brother. Learning later that the rest of her family would be joining Michael, and her desire to distance herself from the rest of the family, she didn't go. On Friday, September 3, several other Jackson family members arrived in Taipei, Taiwan, the Dangerous tour's next stop. Joseph and Katherine, Rebbie, Jackie, Tito and Jermaine all joined Michael. Michael arrived in Taipei on the same day with Elizabeth Taylor and was greeted by hordes of cheering fans who then followed him to his hotel. He later waved to his fans from his penthouse suite at the Taipei Sherwood Hotel. Just after the arrival of his family, Elizabeth Taylor and Larry Fortensky left Taiwan.

Between his two concerts at Taipei's Municipal Stadium, Michael visited a Toys R Us store that closed for two hours for his visit. He spent $4,500 on video games, water pistols and other toys for his nephews who accompanied him to the store. He also spent time with the store manager's children and stopped to paint a picture. Outside the store, photographers crowded around hoping for a shot of the King of Pop. A scuffle ensued between one of the photographers and Michael's bodyguards. The photographer said one of the bodyguards hit him. The bodyguard later apologized. Following the scuffle a politician, Liu Wen-Ching, wanted Michael declared an "undesirable". The President of the Consumers Foundation was upset that other shoppers were removed from the store just for Michael Jackson, "Even a superstar like Michael Jackson should not trample consumer rights just to serve his own shopping needs."

Meanwhile a new document surfaced which looked to be an agreement between the Michael Jackson Organization and another young boy and his mother by which Michael Jackson agreed to pay $600,000 for their silence. The authenticity of this agreement was in question because of some very big problems with it. The supposed contract, dated 1992, was printed on plain paper, no letterhead, was titled "General Agreement", and was not in legal terminology. Also, there is no such thing as the "Michael Jackson Organization"! But certainly if Michael were to enter into such an agreement, his years of experience and his well acknowledged business acumen would certainly dictate he put just such an agreement in writing!

The police said if the document was deemed to be authentic, a separate investigation would be opened to investigate it. No such investigation was ever opened. It does indicate however the lengths some were willing to go to for attention, and in most cases, money.

Two weeks after the story of the allegations against Michael Jackson broke, *A Current Affair* devoted their entire show to Michael Jackson. Host Maureen O'Boyle reported, "There is real fear tonight that the catastrophic publicity of the past two weeks will result in the destruction of a billion dollar empire and the ruin of a man." She failed to admit that this very show was one of the prime sources of that "catastrophic publicity". That if it weren't for her very show and its stories, the whole situation could be seen in a more realistic and rational light and wouldn't have become such a seeming disaster. But that wouldn't earn her show any badly wanted ratings points would it?

O'Boyle would later appear on a talk show to defend her show and her stories, claiming she only reports facts, and is objective. Certainly this particular story, titled, "Michael Jackson: The Curtain Closes" doesn't reflect any sensationalism or negativity.

Michael received some added support from interviews with a former photographer, Dan O'Daud and his former publicist, Norman Winter. O'Daud, who knew if Michael were actually guilty he could have paid the money and avoided the whole scandal, asked, "Does anybody actually think, in their right mind, that a guy with as much money as Michael Jackson has would let something like this occur? I mean does anybody actually think he couldn't cover this up if he wanted to?". O'Daud added that he would trust Michael Jackson with his own son. Norman Winter explained why Michael likes to spend time with children, "He likes to be with kids more than adults because he feels comfortable, he can relax. He feels their not gonna hustle him."

The tour's next stop was Fukoka, Japan. Michael arrived in Fukoka on September 7 and was greeted wildly by fans. He bowed to his fans then boarded a bus for Huis Ten Bosch park where he spent two nights. Michael performed two concerts in Fukoka. The day after his arrival, Michael and his bodyguards boarded boats and travelled along the cost of a reproduction Dutch canal to the Palace, Huis Ten Bosch park's fanciest hotel. Michael also visited a school at a U.S. naval base in Japan.

Michael thrilled 30,000 fans at his September 10th concert. Fans held banners reading, "We Believe You", and "We Believe You Always." There was also one special fan who got to see Michael perform in Japan. Michael had flown a terminally ill Dutch boy, 15 year old Martijn Hendricsen, and his two brothers to Japan. They were driven in a twenty three foot gold limousine to Amsterdam airport to meet Michael Jackson and see the concert. Michael had responded to a request from the Make A Wish Foundation. Martijn, undergoing chemotherapy for cancer, had wished to meet his idol, Michael Jackson.

The September 10, 1993 issue of *Entertainment Weekly* magazine featured Michael Jackson on its cover with the caption, "How Bad?". Inside was a readers poll that indicated Michael's popularity had actually risen since the allegations first become public. Forty three percent of those polled said they saw Michael Jackson in a very favorable or favorable light before the allegations. Since the allegations, that number rose to fifty four percent. Only twelve percent of those polled said they believed the allegations were true, but fifty four percent thought his career and reputation would be tarnished even if they allegations were proven to be false. This seemed to contradict the results given in response to the question, "In light of the allegations, do you think you will be less likely to purchase his music in the future?" to which seventy nine percent responded, "no". Only eight percent of those polled said they would be less likely to purchase the products Michael endorses.

Billboard magazine reported similar findings. Michael's sales and airplay showed no adverse effect due to the unsubstantiated allegations being made against him. His current single, "Will You Be There" was ranked at number seven with a bullet, indicating an increase in sales and airplay, on the Hot 100 singles chart and it was in the top ten, five and at number one on the airplay lists of many stations. Airplay of the song's video remained constant on MTV and VH-1.

Michael's latest single from *Dangerous*, "Will You Be There" entered the top ten of the pop singles chart, at number eight, while Janet's second single from *Janet.*, "If", was at number six. *Billboard* officials predicted a close race for number one between them during the coming weeks, but neither of them made it. "Will You Be There" spent six weeks bouncing back and forth between numbers seven and eight, and "If" peaked at number four.

Over the weekend of September 11 and 12, fans marched in support of Michael Jackson in Hollywood. Flowers and cards were left at his freshly polished star on Hollywood's Walk of Fame. At a time when his latest single was reflecting his real life, asking, "In my darkest hour, In my deepest despair, Will you still care?, Will you be there?", the answer was a resounding "yes".

While his career was not directly affected, the scandal attached to Michael Jackson did take a toll in different ways. It was later announced that Michael Jackson would not be receiving the Scopus Award from the Friends of Hebrew University. While the media liked to print that Michael had been dumped, Michael's publicist announced that he had asked to be withdrawn from consideration. A phone call to the West Coast Friends of Hebrew University confirmed the publicist's statement. The official statement from the university stated:

*Prior to the leak in a show business trade publication of **Daily Variety** that the Hebrew University will seek a replacement for Michael Jackson, the latter had earlier requested the Western Friends of Hebrew University to withdraw his name as recipient of their Scopus Laureate Award on January 29 in Los Angeles. His spokesman also had conveyed at that time the artist's regrets and apologies to the organization for any inconvenience and thanked everyone for understanding and the support extended on his behalf.*

Lois Sheldon, director of a San Diego shelter for women and children with AIDS, decided to withdraw her request to name the facility after Michael Jackson. She had been seeking permission to name the shelter the Michael Jackson Rainbow House. "Because he's been accused of this, I'm going to hold back ... If they called me and said they're going to give me his name, I'd probably give it back until he's cleared of this". Having spent most of her time dealing with people with AIDS, she is probably not used to situations with people being treated unfairly due to a lack of knowledge of their situation. No need to consider here that there was no evidence against Michael, and that he had not been formally charged with so much as jaywalking.

Michael arrived at the next tour stop, Moscow, on September 12, and was greeted by hundreds of fans waving their gloved hands in the air and shouting to him. A banner was held up saying "Siberia Loves You Michael!". The next day Michael left his hotel to do some shopping. He picked up a nineteenth century statue, several paintings and books, and a Russian army officers coat. He also toured the Kremlin museum and armory. The following day, Michael had video shot of himself marching with Russian army soldiers. He did not wear his new coat.

Michael's first show in Moscow was on September 15, at the Lyzhniki Olympic Stadium. Some of the media delighted in reporting that Michael Jackson's concert had not been sold out. What they didn't point out was that the price of the tickets, at $11, was more than most people in Moscow make in a month. They also failed to mention that despite the ticket prices, that 93 percent of the seats were sold. Only seven thousand seats remained unsold for the show at the 100,000 seat stadium.

Michael left Moscow on September 17 for Israel. His concert scheduled for Saturday, September 18 in Tel Aviv was changed to Monday, September 20, so fans wouldn't have to violate the Jewish Sabbath. On Saturday, Michael travelled to Jerusalem for sightseeing but when he visited the ancient Western Wall he was met by screaming protestors who blocked the entrance and threatened to throw chairs at him. He was welcome, however, at Masada, another historic site. It was quite a different scene at his first of two shows in Tel Aviv on Sunday as 80,000 screaming fans jammed into the stadium to see him.

Besides sightseeing, Michael visited child cancer victims in Israel. He also visited Tsirn Army Base.

Meanwhile, the tabloids and talk shows couldn't get enough of the "Michael Jackson Scandal". Soon former employees of Michael's would begin crawling out of the woodwork with inside information on Michael's personal life. This "information" was for sale to the highest bidder, and the tabloid magazines and tabloid TV shows were climbing over each other at the chance to land "the exclusive interview". Whether or not the information was true was not an issue, as long as they had someone to say it was true. First up was Mark and Faye Quindoy, a Filipino husband and wife who had worked as a housekeeper and cook at Neverland from 1989 to 1991. He was a former lawyer. They left their employment at Neverland claiming they were owed $500,000 in overtime pay. If this is an indication of their pay scale, it certainly explains why he stopped practicing law to become a housekeeper! The Quindoys had filed a lawsuit against Michael Jackson for their overdue pay. Later, they claimed they quit because they couldn't stand what they were observing at the ranch. They weren't concerned enough to mention any of it to the authorities though.

The season premiere of *Geraldo* was the first of a several shows devoted to the story. This one even included a year old interview with the Quindoys which at the time only offered slight insights into the personal life of Michael Jackson, but now was being analyzed in a new light by Geraldo Rivera to see if anything said then could now be construed differently. A year earlier, the Quindoys described Michael Jackson as "the shyest person in the world". Other things disclosed in the earlier interview included their observation that each member of Michael's family had visited the ranch with one notable exception, LaToya. They also said Michael had young friends visit him and that they stayed in the "Shirley Temple" room, a separate, enclosed bedroom inside Michael's bedroom. In an effort to get him to eat better, Mrs. Quindoy developed meals named after Michael's zoo animals and Disney characters.

By this time Mark and Faye Quindoy had drastically changed their story. While one year earlier they described Michael to *Geraldo's* audience as a very nice man, they had now suddenly obtained a diary which they held at a press conference which they claimed they had kept while working at the ranch in which they described various questionable acts by "MJ". A very important thing to point out here is that, like so many others in this media fiasco, the Quindoys first told, and sold, their story to *A Current Affair* and did not take anything to the police. And then the police went to them, they did not take their "information" to any authorities. In response to the Quindoy's media blitz with their "diary", two detectives, Federico Sicard and Deborah Linden, flew to Manila to question them. They were found to be worthless as witnesses.

A Current Affair, in their ever objective reporting technique, referred to the Quindoys' press conference as "The press conference that could bring down Michael Jackson forever." Actually the statements made the Quindoys only weakened the case against Michael Jackson, proving people will do and say anything if they think they will profit from it.

The Quindoys were further discredited by their very own nephew. Glen Veneracion, a law student and nephew to the Quindoys, told interviewers his aunt and uncle were opportunists and they were an embarrassment, "I just feel bad that this is happening. I'm ashamed. I'm ashamed to be related to these people. I'm ashamed for the people in our country. It's an embarrassment. It really is." He described the Quindoys antics as a desperate attempt to make money, "What disturbs me the most out of all of this is that they waited so long. Why did it take them three years to come up with these allegations? That's what really is disturbing. If this was true, they should have come out with it a long time ago instead of jumping on the bandwagon. They never said that Michael was a pedophile, they never said that Michael was gay, so I don't know where this is coming from. I find it shocking. It's very disturbing to me."

Veneracion went to Pellicano with his statement and established the lack of credibility of the Quindoys. He answered questions concerning the diary the Quindoys claimed to have kept, "I'm quite sure they wrote that diary to fit in with these allegations. He was gonna get it at any cost. And that's what's coming out now." Veneracion was willing to testify in any court proceedings, "I'd be willing to step forward in a court of law and make these allegations."

Pellicano called the Quindoys "cockroaches and failed extortionist". To prove him wrong, the Quindoys filed another lawsuit, this one suing Pellicano for slander.

Alfonso Ribeiro appeared on *Geraldo*, to say there was never a time when he felt uncomfortable with Michael Jackson. Ribeiro, at the age of twelve, had starred with Michael and the other Jacksons in a Pepsi commercial in 1984. Ribeiro felt like Michael was one of his buddies and felt the allegations were "preposterous". He also disclosed that his own father was offered $100,000 by a tabloid to say anything *negative* about Michael Jackson. Majestik Magnificent, a magician who has known Michael for twelve years and has entertained kids at Neverland, supported Michael vehemently, believing the allegations were the result of an extortion attempt. Magnificent has also worked as a bodyguard for Joseph Jackson. Columnist Florence Anthony also supported Michael. This was but one of many talk show appearances Anthony would make over the next several months to support and defend Michael Jackson. Joseph Jackson phoned Geraldo and expressed his knowledge that his son was guilty of no wrongdoing.

Other of Geraldo's guests were *New York Daily News* columnist Linda Stasi, who claimed to have broke the story four months earlier, reporting that Michael was spending time with a young boy, his sister and mother. *National Enquirer* editor Mike Walker, who published an interview with Chandler and Jordy, stated he felt the boy was believable.

J. Randy Taraborrelli, author of *Michael Jackson: The Magic and the Madness*, also made one of numerous television appearances to express his belief that the allegations were "bogus" and that Michael will surely be cleared of the allegations. He also expressed his surprise by the lack of support from his celebrity friends, Diana Ross, Liza Minnelli, Sophia Loren, Oprah Winfrey, Eddie Murphy, Brooke Shields and Donald Trump.

A crew member who worked on the "Black or White" video for three days, and who wouldn't show his face or give his name, told Geraldo the world exclusive that Michael Jackson was an extremely private person! He also said that Emmanuel Lewis would dance next to Michael, off camera, while filming the video. "Steve", as he was referred, felt this was unusual behavior. It was revealed later that "Steve" was paid for his appearance.

Dr. Bonnie Maslin, a psychotherapist, told Geraldo that you must know a person before making any judgements as to if they are capable of such an act, "I'll ring the neck of any professional who answers that question. Because what you are doing is applying armchair psychology to a person you simply don't know. You're taking gossip and turning it into fact."

Another couple who worked for less than a year at Neverland were also working feverishly to sell their story. Phillipe and Stella Lemarque contacted former porn star Paul Barresi to aid them in selling their story to a London tabloid. The Lemarques were also not above tailoring their story to fit their needs. They initially asked for $100,000 for a story claiming they saw Michael Jackson sexually caress young visitors, including Macaulay Culkin. As their asking price rose, the story changed. When their price increased to $500,000, Michael's hand moved to inside Culkin's pants. Barresi admitted he didn't care if the story was true, he was just helping them sell the story because he was promised a percentage of their selling price.

Maury Povich would also devote several shows to the "Michael Jackson Scandal". The first of which featured a former chauffeur, who appeared in disguise, magician and Jackson friend Majestik Magnificent, *London Sun* editor Piers Morgan, *Sister to Sister* magazine's and Jackson friend, Jamie Foster Brown, *Vibe* magazine's editor Alan Light, and *Hard Copy's* Diane Dimond. Before any discussion of the matter, a poll was taken of the studio audience which showed 84% of the audience members believed Michael Jackson was innocent.

The disguised chauffeur, "Chris", had driven Michael and his young friends to Toys R Us a few times. He stated he never saw any out of the ordinary behavior. Majestik Magnificent reiterated that no one has done more for children than Michael Jackson. Piers Morgan noted he had never heard of any other stories of this nature about Michael Jackson before. He also said that because Michael Jackson is such a massive star, he is put in the position of having to prove his innocence. When the possibility of extortion was mentioned, Morgan immediately responded that there was no evidence of extortion and spent very little time discussing the possibility. However there is no evidence of any molestation, but he was having no problem appearing on a show devoted entirely to that possibility. Alan Light predicted Michael would prevail, that he would come out of it.

Then there was Diane Dimond who pointed out that you don't get a search warrant without proof. She later admitted she didn't know what this "proof" was or why the authorities didn't take this "proof" and file charges against Michael Jackson. Dimond went on to claim her mind was open and defended her show's coverage of the story. "What do you want the media to do when they are confronted with authoritative documents, police reports and allegations of child abuse?" First of all, Dimond wasn't "confronted" with any documents. Her show bought copies of the documents for $10,000.

No one will argue that the media shouldn't cover such a story. Certainly Michael Jackson is a massive superstar and a story such as this can hardly be ignored. Nor should it be. The press has the right and the responsibility to report the facts. Just the facts. They have no such responsibility to distort and manipulate those facts into something they are not to win ratings points. While nobody, no celebrity, not even Michael Jackson, warrants any special considerations when dealing with such allegations, his celebrity certainly shouldn't warrant excessive, undue persecution or harassment either.

Dimond went on to say in the program that people are "innocent until proven guilty but when there are allegations of child abuse, a seed is planted in people's minds that you're guilty. Guilty until you prove your innocence." She failed to admit that her own stories help to plant that seed of doubt.

At the show's conclusion, Povich asked if any member in the audience changed their view after hearing the statements made on the program. Not one person raised their hand.

The Dangerous tour played in Istanbul, Turkey, on September 23 and a September 26 show was scheduled for the Canary Islands. It was announced that proceeds from a show in New Dehli, India, would go to the Ghandi Foundation for Children. Pepsi guaranteed a minimum donation of $160,000.

Upcoming dates in Johannesburg were canceled. A wide variety of reasons for the cancellation were given, including difficulty in moving the show, scheduling problems and continued violence in South Africa. Another reason given was that world tour promoter Marcel Avram, of Mama Concerts, claimed he had no contract with the local promoter, Anant Singh. ANC leader Nelson Mandela was reported to have appealed to Michael not to disappoint his fans but the shows did not go on. Whatever the reason, with the cancellation of these dates, scheduled for September 30 and October 2, Michael took a well deserved break from the tour and spent a few days at Elizabeth Taylor's Swiss chalet.

Back in Hollywood, a Michael Jackson jacket that had been stolen from the Guiness Museum of World Records in Hollywood three weeks earlier, was recovered on September 24. Michael Jackson impersonator Audrey Ruttan had purchased the jacket from a used clothing store, Formula Uno, for $1,000. The store had purchased the jacket from the thief for $100. Ruttan had taken out a loan to buy the jacket but was reimbursed. Ruttan, a big supporter of Jackson's, laid out a banner across Michael's star on the Hollywood Walk of Fame and collected signatures in support of Michael. She collected thousands of signatures within just a few hours.

The September 27 issue of *Forbes* magazine included their annual listing of "The Highest Paid Entertainers". Michael Jackson was listed at number twelve with an estimated two year income of $42 million. Michael's 1992 earnings were estimated at $26 million, and his 1993 earnings were estimated at $16 million.

Also in September, the nominees for induction into the Rock and Roll Hall of Fame were announced. The nominees included the Jackson Five. Later when the actual inductees were chosen, the Jackson Five were not among them. One of the requirements for consideration is that it must be at least twenty five years since the artists' first recording. As such, Michael Jackson, who made his first solo recording in 1971, will be eligible for consideration as a solo artist in 1996.

While continuing the tour and dealing with the unending media attention to his problems, Michael also had problems at home. A blaze in the Los Padres National Forest in October, charred forty thousand acres of land and came within three miles of Neverland Valley before firefighters contained the fire. Just a couple of days later, firefighters entered Neverland to light backfires to stop a wildfire. Officials said the fire was started by a hunter's cigarette.

On October 6, Bert Fields filed a libel suit against the *Globe*. The tabloid had reported in September that Fields had offered hush money to Michael Jackson's accusers. Fields was suing for $10 million.

Despite appearances in the media, there were still some who were firmly in Michael's corner. Sony issued a statement in October reinforcing their support for Michael:

Sony Music's support for Michael Jackson remains unwavering and unconditional. We are heartened by the overwhelming public support for Michael Jackson and widespread skepticism of the allegations brought against him. We are confident the allegations against him are without merit and believe the investigation will exonerate Michael.

Frank Dileo, in his first public statement since being fired as Michael's manager in 1990, supported Michael telling *Rolling Stone*, "I would trust my own children with him, and have...He lived in my house in Encino for seven months. There is no way that he did that. It's not in his nature." Dileo also told *Entertainment Weekly*, "Michael never really had a childhood and I think he is trying to experience it in later life. I would tell him to keep the knowledge that he is innocent and hold his head up." Bruce Swedian, an recording engineer and producer who has worked with Michael for seventeen years, told *Rolling Stone*, "I am mortified and disgusted by what has been reported with no evidence of anything untoward. Michael is one of the most decent people I've ever met in my life. These allegations are preposterous." Michael's former attorney, John Branca, told the same issue of *Rolling Stone*, "If the sense is that Michael was unfairly accused, I think people will empathize with him as a victim to such a degree that is will be a major positive in his career... I think people will be so disgusted, that they'll say, 'Look at this guy. He did nothing wrong and look what the press did to him'. I think he will be a hero." People who have worked closely with Michael for long periods of time knew the allegations couldn't be true.

The October 14 issue of *Rolling Stone* also carried the publication's listing of The 100 Top Music Videos. Michael Jackson had five entries on the list that included the one that undoubtedly echoed his current feelings, "Leave Me Alone", at number eight. "Beat it" was ranked at number twelve, "Thriller" was listed at a surprisingly low number sixteen, "Billie Jean" was number twenty seven on the list, and "Black or White" was his lowest entry on the top 100, at number fifty two.

On Wednesday, October 6, Michael was greeted by hundreds of cheering fans in Argentina. He performed on October 8 in Buenos Aires where thousands of tickets were given out to disadvantaged children.

Another illness forced the cancellation of a show scheduled for October 21 in Chile. Some reports said he was suffering from throat problems, others blamed the illness on drinking tap water. The performance was moved to Saturday. A pulled back muscle was blamed for the cancellation of a show in Lima, Peru.

The October 23 issue of *Billboard* celebrated thirty years in show business for Diana Ross. A special section of the magazine devoted to Ross contained many congratulatory ads, including one that read, "Congratulations! In much love, MJJ Productions" with Michael's Moonwalker logo. This seemed surprisingly cool in comparison to one placed earlier in the same publication for Berry Gordy. Also, it was signed "MJJ Productions" and not by Michael. Ross would be among Michael's close friends who were conspicuously silent during Michael's media hanging. Even while making public appearances to promote her new book, album, and TV movie, she never once even mentioned Michael's name.

The criminal investigation past the mid October date at which the police had earlier said they expected it to be ended. They continued interviewing young boys in hopes of finding somebody to corroborate Jordy's allegations. Eventually questioning forty to sixty boys, and according to some sources, up to one hundred boys, not one corroborated the allegations. The police were questioning every person listed in an address book that was seized in the search of either Michael's Century City condo or at Neverland Valley. The police questioned all young friends of Michael's and their friends in hopes of finding something. They found nothing. The police reportedly even resorted to lying to the young boys in an effort to get them to admit to something. Michael's attorney Bert Fields learned of this and fired off a letter on October 28, to Los Angeles Police Chief Willie Williams:

I am advised that your officers have told frightened youngsters outrageous lies, such as, 'We have nude photos of you', to push them into making accusations against Mr. Jackson. There are, of course, no such photos of these youngsters, and they have no truthful allegations to make. But your officers appear ready to employ any device to generate potential evidence against Mr. Jackson.

Chief Williams' only response was that he was satisfied with the investigation by his officers.

Michael scheduled a visit on October 28, to El Nuevo Reino Aventura amusement park in Mexico, home to Keiko, the whale in *Free Willy*. Michael ended up not making it to the park, but he did pay for five thousand under privileged children to visit the park.

Michael did get out in Mexico to shop at a Mixup Record Store at Pabellon Polanco shopping mall. During his one hour visit, Michael signed autographs and purchased $4,000 worth of laser discs and compact discs. He seemed very comfortable during his visit and even danced in the back of the store.

Seventy thousand fans packed into Aztec Stadium on October 29 were unconcerned about the investigation and shouted, "Michael!, Michael!" Michael kept the hysterical crowd on their feet for more than two hours.

Samuel Jackson, Michael's grandfather, died on October 31, 1993 in a Phoenix nursing home. While much of the press reported he was 100 years old, most sources give Samuel's birthdate as 1903, making him 90 years old at the time of his death. There were rumors that Samuel Jackson was receiving state paid health benefits for the poor. Michael did not leave his tour to attend the funeral services and in fact was recovering from oral surgery the day of the funeral.

Earlier in the month, Michael's thirty five year old cousin, Tony Jackson, died in a car accident. Michael was very close to his cousin and while he wasn't able to return home for the funeral, he did pay all of the funeral expenses.

For their Halloween celebration, Magic Mountain theme park created a light show for their visitors that featured, appropriately enough, "Thriller".

Michael had more problems with fire on November 1st, when fire damaged an office at Neverland. A worker was burned and a Neverland employee was treated for smoke inhalation. The fire was started by a worker using a flammable liquid in refinishing the floor of an office. The fire caused $5,000 to $7,000 damage.

A show scheduled for November 2nd in Mexico City was postponed due to Michael suffering from a toothache. A second show was postponed on November 4th as Michael recovered from oral surgery. He had been hospitalized overnight following the extraction of an abscessed tooth. A performance on November 6th was also postponed as he continued to recover. All three shows were rescheduled for November 7, 9, and 11.

Sony Music Mexico executives Aloysio Reis and Raul Vasquez presented Michael with a double platinum award for sales of *Dangerous* in excess of 500,000 copies in Mexico. Despite his continued legal problems, sales of *Dangerous* increased five hundred percent during his stay there and fans flocked to his concerts. In five shows, the Dangerous tour played to over 500,000 fans in Mexico. His previous three shows in Buenos Aires, Argentina, attracted 240,000 fans, two shows in Sao Paulo, Brazil played to 160,000 fans, and 85,000 fans attended a single show in Santiago, Chile.

Howard Manning, an attorney, flew to Mexico City to take Michael's deposition for a copyright infringement case. Michael, along with Lionel Richie, Quincy Jones, Rod Temperton, and Joe Jackson, were being sued for stealing "The Girl is Mine", "Thriller", and "We Are the World" from two former neighbors of the Jacksons in Gary, Indiana, Reynaud Jones and Robert Smith. Manning spent seven hours deposing Michael for the case on November 8 and November 10. Michael's testimony was videotaped for use in the court case.

The police executed a fourth search warrant in their investigation on November 8, on Hayvenhurst, the Jackson family's Encino home. Although some media outlets reported a nude photo of a young boy was found at the house, a source from the police department said there was nothing found in the boxes of video tapes and photographs taken in the search to incriminate Michael.

It was being reported in the press at this time that the police had obtained a search warrant for Michael Jackson's body. Apparently his accuser had given police a description of Michael Jackson's body, including his genitals. He described blotches on Michael's skin caused from vitiligo, the skin disorder Michael suffers from which destroys the pigmentation of the skin, causing blotching.

Elizabeth Taylor and Larry Fortensky flew to Mexico on November 9th to again be by Michael's side. Michael reportedly called Taylor and was feeling very distressed. After Michael's performance in Mexico on Thursday, November 11, Michael, Elizabeth and Larry never returned to the El Presidente Hotel. They boarded Elizabeth's charted plane and left Mexico. The plane refueled in Toronto, stopped briefly in Iceland, then landed Saturday morning at London's Luton Airport. The plane then left for Switzerland. Michael was seen clearing customs in England but it could not be confirmed where he went from there. Elizabeth Taylor was seen in Switzerland, but Michael was not with her. Then a startling announcement was made.

4

Where's Michael?

The remaining dates of the Dangerous tour were canceled and Michael was reported to be seeking treatment for a dependency on painkillers. An audio taped message was released to the press in which Michael explained the cancellation of the tour and his need for treatment:

As I left on this tour, I had been the target of an extortion attempt, and shortly thereafter was accused of horrifying and outrageous conduct.

I was humiliated, embarrassed, hurt and suffering great pain in my heart. The pressure resulting from these false allegations coupled with the incredible energy necessary for me to perform caused so much distress that it left me physically and emotionally exhausted. I became

*increasingly more dependent on the painkillers to get me
through the days of the tour.   My friends and doctors
advised me to seek professional guidance immediately in
order to eliminate what has become an addiction.   It is
time for me to acknowledge my need for treatment in order
to regain my health.   I realize that completing the tour is
no longer possible and I must cancel the remaining dates.
I know I can overcome the problem and will be stronger
from the experience."*

The painkillers had been prescribed for Michael
after he had undergone surgery on the back of his scalp
in July.   The surgery was to repair scar tissue caused
from the burn he received while filming a Pepsi commercial in 1984.   Although the accident happened years
ago, he still receives regular treatment from its effects.
Michael's   virtual   disappearance   pushed   the
already frenzied media into overdrive.   Rumors of every
sort imaginable came from literally all over the world.
Speculation on his whereabouts included Elton John's
house in London, Elizabeth Taylor's chalet in Gstaad,
Switzerland, a resort in the French Alps, a hospital in
Canada, a hospital in Connecticut, a facility in Kansas,
and his own ranch in Santa Barbara.   One British
tabloid, the *Daily Mirror,* held a "Spot the Jacko" contest
offering readers a vacation to Disney World if they
could correctly predict where Michael Jackson would
appear next.   The most widely believed location was the
Charter Nightingale Clinic in London.   Many sources
reported Michael and five bodyguards were occupying
the hospital's entire fourth floor.   He was said to be
receiving treatment by Dr. Beauchamp Colclough, who
had been recommended to Michael by Elton John.   Dr.
Colclough   had   treated   Elton   John   for   dependency

problems. The hospital refused to confirm whether or not Michael was there.

Elton John responded to the rumors that Michael Jackson was staying at his house when he was in London to accept a music award. Elton told the crowd, "Michael says,'hi', I would have brought him with me but he's busy hovering (vacuuming) his fucking room!" Actually Michael had spent a short time, about two days, at Elton's house before moving to the Charter Clinic.

Wherever he was, Michael seemed intent on staying out of sight. His attorneys would not comment on his location, neither would Elizabeth Taylor, who had been instrumental in helping Michael get out of Mexico to receive treatment. Michael Jackson impersonators, presumably hired by the Jackson camp, began popping up in London, and throughout Europe throwing photographers and reporters off track. Reporters in London staked out hotels, hospitals, Toys R Us stores and zoos hoping to be the one to finally find Michael Jackson. They found nothing.

Regardless if they didn't know where he was, the tabloids continued churning out stories claiming they knew not only where he was, put what his plans were. The *Sunday Express* headline read, "Drug Treatment Star Faces Life on the Run". The ever accurate and ethical *News of the World* ran the headline, "Hunt for Jacko the Fugitive". Many stories claimed Michael Jackson would never return to the United States, living the rest of his life in hiding somewhere in Europe. Others said Michael panicked and left Mexico fearing he would be arrested if he went to the tour's next stop, Puerto Rico, which is U.S. territory. Other rumors being treated by some media outlets as fact included Michael preparing to come back to the U.S. to turn himself in, others had him on the verge of suicide. The most outrageous stories had Michael hiding out in Europe to undergo cosmetic surgery on his genitals so his appearance would no longer match the description the boy had given to police. Virtually all the tabloid stories and some of the more legitimate news sources cast doubt on Michael's painkiller dependency.

While Michael was out of sight recovering, *A Current Affair* continued to air stories containing statements like, "Following Michael Jackson down the road to ruin" and "How key moments and mistakes destroyed an idol". How was Michael Jackson ruined? When was he ever destroyed? Any statements made by representatives of this scandal ridden show that it is objective and they only report the facts are absurd.

Helping to fuel the latest media frenzy was Eddie Reynoza, who said he was one of the dancers in the "Thriller" video. Reynoza, who admitted he hadn't heard from Michael in ages, claimed Michael Jackson called him on November 18 from Switzerland and said he was never returning to the U.S. and he was transferring all his assets to Switzerland. While he said he taped the alleged fourteen minute conversation, Reynoza is reported to have only ever played a very small portion of the tape for the press, in which "Michael' sounds very drowsy. Consider the logic in Reynoza's claims. After the most famous person in the world meticulously arranges to be indiscreetly flown out of Mexico to God only knows where, landing at least three times, in Canada, England and Switzerland, leaving them all as possibilities of his whereabouts, and possibly hiring Michael Jackson impersonators to throw off the media, the most logical thing to do would be to immediately call someone in the United States that you knew ten years ago and tell them exactly where you are and what your future plans are. Not long after garnering his fifteen minutes of fame, Reynoza's statements were shown to be wrong when Michael did indeed return to the United States. Actually, while Reynoza claimed he met Michael while working on the "Thriller" video and that they struck up a friendship, Michael does not know who he is.

The Monday following the cancellation of the tour, on November 15, Bert Fields held a press conference and explained that Michael Jackson was indeed receiving treatment for a painkiller dependency and they expected the treatment to take six to eight weeks. Fields did concede that Michael Jackson was "barely able to function on an intellectual level." He would not disclose Michael's location and wouldn't even confirm that he was still on Earth! But he did explain that if he chose to return to the U.S. for treatment it would have been impossible to keep his location a secret and he would have never gotten a moments peace from the media:

If we put Michael Jackson to be cured in the United States there is no way in the world that we could have kept the location a secret. There is no way in the world that we could have avoided the media being all around that facility. The fly overs by helicopter, the overzealous fans parachuting into the gardens and things like that, so we decided we would be better off in a place other than the United States.

Fields added that, "He has no intention of avoiding coming to the U.S."

Additional doubt was cast on Michael's painkiller dependency by Howard Manning Jr. who had deposed

Michael in Mexico just before the cancellation of the tour. Manning had deposed Michael in connection with another copyright case in 1989. He told the media that Michael was articulate, could remember details of writing songs with no problem, and he described him as a "coherent, sharp witness".

We became familiar with his brightness. This man knows pretty much about the business. He knows and can recall a good deal about songs he's written, or not written, that goes back years. There was no difference in that performance last week, no difference between that and 1989.

Manning added, "We were not informed of any addiction problem. We did not see any evidence of an addiction problem. The witness was alert, he didn't slur. He answered questions just as he had in 1989." Actually, Bert Fields felt Michael was in no condition to be deposed, but a motion to delay the proceedings had been denied and they had no choice but to continue with the deposition. When tape of Michael's deposition was later viewed in court, and shown on numerous newscasts, it very evident that Michael was indeed very drowsy, had difficulty concentrating, and his speech was slurred at times.

In a complete turn-a-round from just two months earlier, Jack Gordon, LaToya's manager and husband, told the press that he knew Michael was not addicted to drugs at all. He knew this very inside information because, he claimed, Michael had told this to LaToya! Certainly the wisest move on Michael's behalf, were he using the addiction story as an excuse to remain out of the U.S., would be to immediately share this information with LaToya. Of all the people around him, he would certainly turn first to his sister, who he hasn't spoken to in six years.

When the allegations against Michael first became public, Pepsi continued sponsorship of the Dangerous tour and said they supported Michael. Their support weakened dramatically and quickly and they soon developed a wait and see attitude. In what is quite possibly the worst cola decision since New Coke, Pepsi announced on November 14, 1994 that their relationship with Michael Jackson was over. Pepsico spokesman Gary Hemphill said Pepsi's sponsorship was to end when the tour did, so the ending of the tour means, "we no longer have a relationship."

Over their ten year relationship, Michael Jackson's advertisements for Pepsi earned the cola giant approximately $500 million in additional sales. This is just a small indication of Michael's deep and widespread influence on his fans. With Pepsi's announcement, fan clubs and fan magazines around the world urged members to boycott all Pepsi products and to write to the company. Certainly it was no coincidence when within a few weeks, Coke announced a twenty percent increase in sales.

Pepsi claimed in their statement that their relationship with Michael Jackson was ended because the tour had ended. If this were actually the case, no formal announcement would be necessary. It would logically follow that Pepsi could no longer sponsor a tour that was no longer in existence. Obviously, Pepsi wanted to publicly distance themselves from Michael Jackson.

In a follow up phone call to Pepsi, it was said that no formal announcement of their decision to drop

Michael Jackson was made but in fact the press contacted Pepsi on a Saturday and the only person there at the time, Gary Hemphill, refused to give a statement because they had yet to be contacted by Michael Jackson or his representatives. When he was pressed for a statement and was asked his reaction to the cancellation of the tour, Hemphill replied that the ending of the tour meant, "We no longer have a relationship." Pepsi spokeswoman Christine Jones said this statement was then misinterpreted by the wire service as Pepsi was dropping Michael Jackson because of his legal problems and, according to Jones, Pepsi would never do that. She claimed, because Pepsi doesn't usually continue with one celebrity pitchman for so long, if asked if Pepsi were going to continue with Michael Jackson after the conclusion of the Victory tour in 1984, they would have said no. They would have answered similarly after the completion of the Bad tour in 1988, and were doing so now with the ending of the Dangerous tour. She said this "misunderstanding" of Pepsi's announcement by the media was not corrected with a subsequent statement because if Pepsi issued an unsolicited statement, it would not be picked up by any news wire service. It is impossible to believe however that in regards to the "Michael Jackson Scandal", *any* detail was being ignored by the media. Certainly a statement issued by the tour's sponsor would be considered to be rather significant and newsworthy.

Pepsi has a history of suddenly dropping their celebrity pitchman. Madonna was immediately dropped after only one airing of her Pepsi commercial due to controversy over her latest video. Her "Like A Prayer" video, with her dancing scantily clad in front of burning crosses, shocked and offended many viewers. Mike

Tyson was also dropped by Pepsi following his stormy breakup with his wife Robin Givens and charges that he had beaten her.

Many other celebrity pitchmen have been dropped by advertisers because of negative circumstances. Burt Reynolds was suddenly dropped by the Florida Citrus Commission from his Florida orange juice commercials following his very public breakup with his wife Loni Anderson. During the media circus surrounding their breakup, Reynolds admitted he had had an affair. Converse ended their relationship with basketball star Magic Johnson after he announced he was HIV positive. However, one crucial fact seems to be consistently ignored in all of this, Michael had not been charged with anything. Whether it was right or wrong, ethical or not, to drop the other celebrities in these other situations is debatable, but the events or situations that prompted the decisions actually *did* happen; Madonna did offend viewers and Mike Tyson did have a bitter, public breakup with his wife as did Burt Reynolds. Magic Johnson publicly admitted he did test positive for HIV, the virus that causes AIDS. Michael Jackson consistently expressed confidence the investigation against him would prove his innocence and there was no evidence or supporting testimony to suggest Michael Jackson was guilty of anything. He was dropped solely on unsubstantiated allegations and nothing more.

There was also widespread belief in Michael's innocence among the general public and widespread disgust at how he was being treated by the media. Letters were sent to magazine publications, including *People, Entertainment Weekly,* and *Newsweek,* in response to stories on "The Michael Jackson Scandal", the majority of which were supportive of Michael. Many expressed their view that Michael Jackson had been tried and convicted by the media while there were no charges against him.   Volumes of newspaper and magazine articles and stories from tabloid TV shows, after rambling on with potentially damaging statements from either the reporter or writer themselves or from former Neverland employees, frequently ended with a one sentence statement recognizing the fact that there were no charges against Michael. They would not let a little thing like there being no evidence on which to base formal charges stand in their way of reporting some dirt on a superstar.

While Pepsi deserted Michael, Sony did not. On November 17, Sony issued a statement to the press expressing their support for Michael during his legal battles and his health problems, "Michael Jackson's unique position as a world class artist and humanitarian is as important to Sony as it is to the tens of millions around the globe who have been touched by his art and his faith." Sony further commended Michael and his "... personal courage in facing up to the pain of addiction and the difficult path to full recovery that lies ahead. We will stand behind him every step of the way with all the unconditional support and encouragement we can provide."

During the dedication of The Elizabeth Taylor Medical Center, an AIDS center in Washington D.C., Elizabeth Taylor spoke of Michael and her efforts to help him:

I travelled to Mexico City, where I saw for myself that Michael was in desperate need of specialized medical attention. I have suffered and dealt with the same kind of medical problems now affecting my friend, Michael Jackson. Because of that and because of our friendship, when Michael's doctor called to ask if I would help, I was glad to intervene. Because of my own experience with addiction to prescription medicines, I was able to make a number of calls in search of the best and most appropriate treatment for Michael, and he is now undergoing such treatment in Europe.

She refused to say where Michael was receiving treatment, only that he was in Europe:

Because of my regard for him and my concern for his health, I will continue to be silent on these matters.

She also refused to comment on the molestation allegations:

As this is a matter now in the hands of lawyers it would inappropriate for me to comment on it and I will not do so. I will only repeat that I am a friend of Michael Jackson's and I love him like a son, and I support him with all my heart.

While Michael was being treated for his painkiller dependency, *Hard Copy's* Diane Dimond learned there may be new accusers in the case, this being announced on the heels of the Los Angeles Police Department confirming just the opposite, that they were investigating the allegations of only the one boy. Dimonds' story, an illustration of her objectivity and to show she has no preconceived notions or motives, was titled, "Life On The Run". A similar story aired by *A Current Affair* was called "Michael Jackson: The Fugitive". This blatantly

wrong. Michael had not been charged with anything.
There was no warrant for his arrest. Regardless if it
were thought he was guilty or not, he could not be
considered a fugitive.

Michael's treatment delayed the scheduled taping
of the *Jackson Family Honors* special. Originally
planned to tape on December 10 in Atlantic City, it was
now postponed until February 5, and moved to Las
Vegas, when Michael would be able to participate. This
date was later changed again, to February 19, at the
MGM Grand Garden in Las Vegas. While Michael
confirmed he would attend, LaToya's appearance was in
question, and would remain so until hours before the
taping. The family said LaToya was invited, but had not
yet responded. LaToya claimed she had never been
invited, but wouldn't attend anyway because it would
amount to, in her mind, condoning child abuse, referring
to the abuse she claims she suffered from her father. In
announcing these changes, Jermaine also issued a
statement to the press on behalf of the Jackson family
reiterating their support for Michael:

*At the commencement of the investigation of
Michael, our entire family issued a statement of love and
unequivocal support. Today, we confirm that love and
support and will always stand firmly at his side. We are
confident that his dignity and humanity will prevail.*

Michael Jackson's millions of devoted fans
around the world were standing solidly behind Michael
too. They were not about to allow the media's bashing
of Michael Jackson go unchecked and they were very
eager to let Pepsi, Sony, and Michael Jackson himself
know exactly how they felt. Michael Jackson fan clubs

and fan magazines, such as Lori Byler's Michael Jackson Observer Fan Club, Carol Armstrong's Magic World of Michael Jackson and Adrian Grant's *Off The Wall* magazine, encouraged members to actively show their support for Michael. Fans wrote Sony expressing their support for Michael, and they wrote Pepsi condemning their decision to drop him. Pepsi, and all Pepsi products, were vigorously boycotted. Fans were encouraged to write newspapers and TV networks demanding fair coverage of the story. Michael Jackson albums were repurchased by fans to show their support for him, and of course, Michael himself received a flood of cards, letters and flowers, white roses, as a symbol of innocence.

Lori Byler granted numerous interviews in solid support of Michael Jackson. Local television news crews covered her club's Michaelfest, an annual gathering of club members, held this year in Denver on August 29, Michael's birthday. The Michael Jackson International Fan Club, in response to a deluge of letters and calls from fans asking how they could help support Michael, began selling "I Believe in Michael" t-shirts.

As skepticism about Michael's painkiller dependency ran rampant for days on end, there was finally, on November 22, a statement released by the doctor who was treating Michael. Dr. Beauchamp Colclough sent a letter to the press to "refute any suggestion that Mr. Jackson is 'hiding out' or seeking any other care other than the program for analgesia abuse." Dr. Colclough addressed suggestions that Michael was undergoing cosmetic surgery, and that he was suicidal, saying further that "no other medical, surgical or psychological condition exists":

Mr. Jackson was presented to me on Friday evening, 12th November 1993 by Dr. David Forecast and Miss Elizabeth Taylor, after their trip from Mexico City... An initial assessment of Mr. Jackson's condition was made. A detoxification program was completed today. After an initial 36 hours, Mr. Jackson's started an intensive program of group therapy and one-to-one therapy with myself.

I confirm that no other medical, surgical, or psychological condition exits. I present this statement to strongly refute any suggestion that Mr. Jackson is 'hiding out' or seeking any other care.

This letter proved the media wrong in their statements that Michael was not addicted to drugs and was afraid to return to the U.S. Some were going so far as predicting he would never return. Others said he was undergoing cosmetic surgery so when he did return, nobody would be able to recognize him! While these are ridiculous statements to make, people do believe them when they see them in black and white, so they needed to be addressed. After all the truly far out and unbelievable garbage being printed, the media was shown to be wrong. It would not be the last time Michael Jackson would show the media, and the world, that they were wrong and he was much stronger than they knew.

The ending of the Dangerous tour and Michael's admission he was seeking treatment for a dependency problem only added fuel to the flames of controversy and scandal being fed by the tabloid and scandal shows. Geraldo Rivera displayed perhaps the worst taste to date with a show devoted to putting on a mock trial of Michael Jackson. Michael had not been charged with anything and Geraldo was already putting together a trail! A jury composed of audience members heard arguments from New York attorney Raoul Felder, acting as a defense attorney, and from New York attorney Ruth Walden who acted as the prosecuting attorney. Some witnesses were actually present on the show, other testimony was taken from footage of earlier interviews or press conferences. Among the witnesses called for the prosecution were a tape of the Quindoys, a portion of a press conference held by Gloria Allred at the beginning of the investigation, Ginny Klein, a sex abuse expert, who said she couldn't make any generalizations without knowing him, Mike Walker, editor of the *National Enquirer*, whose "magazine" featured an interview with Evan Chandler. A member of Michael's crew, who didn't give his name and wore a disguise, related that Michael's relationships with youngsters was the talk of the crew. He also admitted he at no time saw any sexual touching and no sexual overtures.

The defense witnesses included Tim Whitehead, Michael's cousin who is very close to Michael, who told the jury he had been offered $100,000 to say that Michael is gay. He refused and said he has never seen any behavior that could be construed as child abuse. Choreographer Michael Peters, who has known Michael for years and has worked on videos for "Thriller" and "Beat It" appeared on the program to say he never saw any improper behavior on Michael's part with any children. This was echoed by Steve Manning who also appeared on the program to defend Michael. Taped interviews with Elizabeth Taylor and Alfonso Reibero each stated their trust in Michael's integrity and their belief that the allegations were preposterous. Michael's parents, Katherine, from a press conference, and Joseph, who phoned Geraldo, each defended their son. A young female friend of Michael's, Amanda Porter, appeared on the program to support her idol and friend. Amanda's mother, Carole Nowicki, who also has a young son, said she would trust Michael with her son's life.

At the end of the show, the "jury" found there was insufficient evidence to find Michael Jackson guilty of child molestation. *Geraldo's* title as the lowest of the scandal-mongering talk shows would be short lived, but it would take *A Current Affair* to go even lower.

Superior Court Judge David M. Rothman, on November 23, denied a request filed by Michael's attorneys to postpone the civil suit until the criminal proceedings were completed. The judge ruled that the boy's right to a speedy trial prevailed over Michael Jackson's request to delay the proceedings and set a court date for March 21, 1994. In setting the court date, Rothman followed California's 120 day speedy trial rule, that requires a trial date within 120 days when the alleged victim is under fourteen. In the judge's view, this rule superseded Michael Jackson's request to delay the civil suit until his name was cleared in the criminal investigation. Bert Fields stated that Michael wanted to testify and clear his name in the criminal proceedings before the civil trial. That would of course hurt the prosecution's case in the civil suit.

Rothman ordered Michael to give a deposition in the case by January 31, 1994. The request for the delay had been filed on October 29 by Bert Fields so they wouldn't have the criminal investigation and the civil suit to contend with simultaneously. At the time of the request, the judge ordered that no interviews be conducted in connection with the civil case until after his decision on November 23. Again the press went off half cocked reporting that Michael's attorneys wanted to delay the civil case for six years, at which time the statute of limitations on the criminal case would have run out. Actually they asked for it to be held until the criminal investigation was completed. (Which by the way it was going, appeared that it would take longer than six years!)

During the November 23 hearing, Bert Fields told the court "a grand jury convened already in Santa Barbara County and are about to take evidence, if they haven't already started, and that means we should expect a charging decision very, very soon." This information given to Fields turned out to be false and Fields' statement was immediately recanted by co-counsel Howard Weitzman. The grand jury session had not actually been called.

On the music front, the November release of Michael Jackson's *Greatest Hits* album was postponed because Michael had not yet finished recording the two new songs to be included on the album. The album was now scheduled for release in mid 1994. But that didn't mean there wouldn't be new Michael Jackson products on the market for Christmas. On November 23, *Dangerous: The Short Films*, a collection of videos from the *Dangerous* album was released. The video cassette was originally scheduled for release in January 1993 but, as has become a pattern with new Michael Jackson products, it was delayed as Michael was constantly making changes. Included was the complete version of "Black or White" which had been enhanced to now include racial slurs and a swastika painted on the car windows and store front window that Michael smashes out. News footage of the uproar that followed the premiere of the video showed the intense attention that was paid to the first video released from the album. And it pointed out that even if you didn't care Michael Jackson had a new album out, you couldn't take your eyes off of the video. Following "Black or White" is a sneak peak at the making of the video and the fun Michael had on the set with stink bombs and inciting a whipped cream fight with the children appearing in the video and director John Landis. There is also behind the scenes footage of "Remember the Time", "In the Closet" and "Jam".

In addition to the videos from the album, *The Short Films* also has footage of Michael's tours and award ceremonies. The segment of the 1993 Grammy Awards is included with Janet presenting Michael with the Grammy Legend Award, and Michael proving once and for all that he and Janet "really are two different people!" The presentation of the 1993 NAACP Entertainer of the Year Award to Michael Jackson is also included on *Dangerous: The Short Films.* Footage from two Pepsi commercials that never aired in the United States is on the cassette with Michael playing piano with a younger version of himself in the background. Also the video for "Who Is It" that was only released in Europe is finally seen by his U.S. fans. Instead of the video for "Will You Be There" footage from concerts is combined with Michael's performance of the song on *MTV 10*, a television special commemorating the tenth anniversary of MTV. Two versions of "Heal the World" are included, the song's video and Michael's performance at the 1993 Super Bowl.

Michael's most recent video, "Gone Too Soon", his tribute to his friend Ryan White, is on the video cassette as well. The song was later issued as a cassette single coinciding with the creation of the Ryan White Foundation.

Epic released the video package betting Michael-mania was still alive and well. They were right. *Dangerous: The Short Films* was reported to be selling strongly, with some outlets reporting they couldn't keep it on the shelves. *Dangerous: The Short Films* debuted on *Billboard's* Top Music Video chart at number four, where it spent several months in the top five.

Free Willy, new on home video just a few days earlier, spent several months in the top five of *Billboard's* Top Video Sales chart, peaking at number two where it spent nine weeks. The video for "Will You Be There" was included at the beginning of the movie. *Free Willy* ended 1993 as the number ten top grossing movie of the year, grossing $77 million. Later the film was honored with a Genesis Award for Motion Picture of the Year. The Genesis Awards are in given in recognition of a film's efforts to address animal issues.

Also out in time for Christmas was *Pigtails and Frog Legs*, a holiday cookbook produced by the Neiman Marcus stores. The book included a foreword by Michael Jackson titled "Nourish This Child", in which he expressed his feelings of how a mother shows her love for her child in preparing food for her child:

> *To a child, food is something special. It isn't just a delicious taste or the vitamins that build a healthy body. Food is love and caring, security and hope - all the things that a food family can provide. Remember when you were little and your mother made a pie for you? When she cut a slice and put it on your plate, she was giving you a bit of herself, in the form of her love. She made you feel safe and wanted. She made your hunger go away, and when you were full and satisfied, everything seemed all right. Because that satisfied feeling was in the pie, you were*

nourished from a deep level. Food is something we all need physically, but so is the love, the deeper nourishment, that turns us into who we are.

Think about how necessary it is to nourish a child with a bit of yourself when you use this book. It is full of delicious things. Every recipe has an extra ingredient of caring, because the people who wrote them were thinking of the children. They were especially thinking of those who aren't able to take nourishment for granted because they are poor, sick, or disabled. These are the children who need food to heal. The theme of "Heal the World", which has been close to my heart, is the central theme of this book also. Here are recipes for the spirit. Please make them with that in mind. Your child is growing spirit that can be knit strong with love. When you break an egg and measure a cup of flour, you are magically mixing the gift of life. The food's proteins and minerals will turn into bones and muscles, but your feeling as you cook will turn directly into a soul.

It makes me happy to think that the needs of children's spirits are at last becoming important in this world. Children have no power to end wars directly or to mend age-old differences. All they can do is be themselves, to shine with gratitude and joy when love is turned their way. Yet isn't that ultimately the greatest power? In the eyes of a child you become the source of joy, which lifts you into the special category of caregiver and life-provider. You may think that your apple pie has only sugar and spice in it. A child is wiser-with the first bite, he knows that this special dish is the essence of you love. Enjoy!

Michael Jackson
Heal the World Foundation

According to Neiman Marcus spokeswoman Liz Barrett, sales of the book were unaffected by Michael's legal situation.

The business side of Michael's life was also flourishing. On November 24, it was announced that he had just closed the biggest music publishing deal in history. He had agreed to let EMI Music manage his music publishing company, ATV Music. The total value of the deal was reported to be $200 million, with Michael getting $100 million in advance. As part of the five year deal, EMI agreed to provide funds with which to acquire other music catalogs and then share ownership with Michael Jackson, including Jobete Music, Berry Gordy's catalog of Motown classics. Michael's entire music publishing catalog, including songs he has written, is estimated at $500 million.

ATV Music was originally with EMI when Michael first purchased the catalog in 1985. He later moved the catalog to MCA Music in a deal that expired on December 31, 1993. The ATV catalog contains, in addition to 251 Lennon and McCartney/Beatle compositions, songs by Elvis Presley, Little Richard, the Pointer Sisters, Kenny Rogers, and others.

Us magazine published a readers poll in its November issue that had Michael Jackson mentioned in several categories. He was listed third on the list as the Most Overexposed Celebrity, and on the list for whose comeback was least welcome. A favorite now for over a decade, "Thriller" was voted as the second Best Music Video, sandwiched between the recent releases, "That's The Way Love Goes" by Janet Jackson, and Aerosmith's "Living on the Edge". Michael and Janet Jackson headed the reader's choices for the duet they would most like to see. Michael Jackson and Madonna were the readers' second choice.

Just when it seemed Michael's legal problems had peaked, five former security guards that had worked at Hayvenhurst filed a lawsuit against Michael Jackson, MJJ Productions, Anthony Pellicano, Norma Staikos and others, on November 22 claiming they were fired because they "knew too much." The suit asked for unspecified monetary damages and charged Michael and the others with conspiracy, harassment, wiretapping, and surveillance.

The guards, Leroy Thomas, Morris Williams, Donald Starks, Fred Hammond and Aaron White, had been fired in February, 1993. The guards were employed by the Jacksons and actually did not even work for Michael. When they were laid off, one of the guards, Morris Williams, repeatedly called journalist and Jackson friend Florence Anthony asking to get in contact with Michael. He said he knew Michael did not know he had lost his job and knew Michael would help him get it back. Michael complied and did get him his job back. Later he was laid off again. The guards were replaced by a less costly security company which provides guards and pays their vacation and insurance costs.

One of the guards, Leroy Thomas, alleged he was ordered by Michael to go to his private bathroom and destroy a nude photo of a young boy. As would be the case with other former employees of Michael's, suddenly appearing on TV claiming they had some critical information about Michael Jackson, their stories just didn't make much sense. They seemed to raise more questions about their own credibility than cast any doubt on Michael's innocence. This didn't prevent *Hard Copy* or *A Current Affair* from exploiting the stories of course. In fact, the most serious damage to Michael Jackson didn't come from what these former employees had to say, but the attention they were given by the tabloid media.

Nervous that these guards "knew too much" about his private life, Michael naturally disclosed to one of them where he hid his key, and asked him to go to his private bathroom, take down a polaroid picture of a naked boy and destroy it. Assuming there ever was any such picture, if Michael had something so potentially damaging to hide and was worried these guards were too well informed about his personal life, he would have certainly destroyed it himself. There would be no need at all to let a soul know the photo ever existed.

The guards claimed further that Michael would frequently have young guests visit with him at the Encino estate, not exactly a state secret. They also "revealed" that Michael would call them to see if his parents were home before coming to the house, staying away if they were home. This is also not a very well guarded secret. J. Randy Taraborrelli wrote in his biography of Michael Jackson that Michael would frequently turn away from the house if he saw his parents', or especially his father's, car was in the drive. Statements by these former guards that they were asked to hold young boys in the guard house until Joe and Katherine left or went to bed, and Michael sent for them is debatable. According to Katherine, one of the young boys the guards claim they were asked to hold was John Lennon's son, Sean, who has been friends with Michael for years and has visited with Michael frequently, with Katherine fully aware he was there.

Despite what the tabloids tried to derive from the guards' statements, they did admit they never witnessed Michael molest anybody, they never witnessed any improper behavior by Michael around his guests, and they never saw one unhappy visitor at Hayvenhurst. Some very significant facts must be considered in connection with these statements besides the important questions of the credibility of their claims. First, they were paid handsomely for their public statements. *Hard Copy* had paid the guards a reported $150,000 for their story. Leroy Thomas, Fred Hammond and Morris Williams also made the rounds to talk shows to discuss what they "knew". Also, if these guards had important suspicions or concerns about Michael's behavior, why did they not contact the police at the time rather than turning up on a long line of talk shows some ten months later?

Actually this was the second lawsuit filed by the guards. They had lost an earlier lawsuit filed shortly after their dismissal.

Following the guards' TV appearances, they began to claim they were being harassed. One was reportedly nearly hit by a car, the window of a car dealership where one is now employed was shot at, and one claimed he was being followed. It was beginning to look like you couldn't make inflammatory and potentially damaging claims against the world's most loved superstar, collect your fees, and live in peace!

A few weeks later another former employee came forward with supposedly more damaging information on Michael. Branca Francia worked as a maid at Neverland Valley from 1988 to 1991. She claimed she quit in disgust in 1991. It was later learned she had in fact been fired. In December, 1993, she couldn't hold this "information" in any longer and just had to tell it to Diane Dimond of *Hard Copy*. She didn't fare as well as the guards however, she was only paid $20,000 for her story. But it was still in excess of a year's salary for her. Only after her exclusive interview with the tabloid TV show did she give a deposition for the civil suit.

Hard Copy built her up as trusted confident of Michael Jackson's when actually the maid, who had been fired two years earlier, hardly knew Michael Jackson.

Francia's story has more holes in it than that of the five guards. Among her claims were instances of her entering Michael's bedroom to find him in the shower with a young boy. And, according to the interview that was aired on TV, she suspected there was possible molestation of her own son. Again the question is raised of why, upon witnessing these things, did she not go directly to the police? Why would she wait two years to speak out, especially if she suspected abuse of *her own son?*

The claims Francia made simply do not fit. It was said that the floor outside Michael's bedroom was wired, so sounds or footsteps in the hallway were amplified, letting him be aware someone was coming. Why would he then allow anyone to enter his room if he were in the shower, whether alone or with another person? Michael's intense shyness and self conscious-ness must also be considered here. This is a person who wears sunglasses and sometimes a surgical mask in public so people can't see his face. As a teenager he had acne on his face that caused so much distress for him that he stopped looking at people in the eye, and he would wash his face in the dark so he wouldn't have to look at his own reflection in the mirror. That hardly sounds like someone who would allow his household staff to parade around his bathroom while he was naked. In addition to his own shyness and modesty, Michael suffers from vitiligo which destroys the pigmentation of the skin, causing blotching. Sufferers of vitiligo tend to become very self conscious of the blotching. So, in addition to his already extreme shyness, and his skin disorder, Michael is supposed to have allowed his housekeeper to not only see him naked in the shower, but allowed her to enter his private quarters when he was in the shower with a young boy!

During the course of the interview, Francia said Michael would give her bonuses; gifts and cash, in return for her to lie to Katherine Jackson, telling her Michael wasn't home when in fact he was. Francia said in return for these "bonuses", she didn't mind lying to Mrs. Jackson for Michael. But her statements here are supposed to be believable even though she accepted $20,000 to say them! She accepted money to lie before but this was the truth!

It is very possible however that Francia's deposition given for the civil suit differed drastically from her TV interview. Following the airing of the interview, Francia complained that it had been edited, making it appear that she said things that she didn't actually say. During the interview, Dimond asked very leading questions, almost forcing allegations from Francia.

Francia's claims were refuted by several other former employees. Lary Glenn Anderson, a former security guard at Neverland Valley Ranch, said he "never saw Jackson doing anything out of line with the boys who were overnight guests. He's shy; he doesn't undress in front of boys." Two important points about his comments are, first, he wasn't paid for his comments. Secondly, they simply make sense, they fit in with Michael's character and personality. Shanda Lujan worked as a maid at Neverland Valley the same time as Blanca Francia and part of her duties involved entering

Michael's private room. Lujan refuted Blanca's claims and added, "I think it's ridiculous. He was great with kids. I think he'd make a very good father. He's just wonderful with them." Another maid, Francin Orosco, said of Francia, "You could tell a lot that she had a little crush on him, very jealous of the other housekeepers. She didn't want no one close to Michael. There's a lot of jealously there."

As the tabloid media never missed an opportunity to exploit the Michael Jackson story, the media itself took several poundings by people outraged at their unfair handling of the story and their apparent assumption that Michael was guilty. One of those who stepped up to publicly denounce the media was oscar winning actor Maximilian Schell. Schell paid to have a one page hand written letter to Michael published on the back page of the *Hollywood Reporter:*

To Michael Jackson (Somewhere on this planet)
Dear Michael,
I am deeply ashamed - for the press, for the media, for the world. I don't know you - we met only once on one of those award dinners (Entertainer of the Decade). We shook hands - you were kind and polite. I don't think you knew who I was. How should you? Our world's are too far apart - (I am more "classical" minded -) but I looked into your eyes - they were kind.

You are a great artist and I admire you. My little daughter (she is 4 1/2) loves you! Deeply - she even wants to marry you! ("But he never calls me!") She imitates you all the time - and quite well.

We all love you. I would like her more to listen to Mozart but she loves YOU! AND I RESPECT HER TASTE! - That you survive this avalanche of dirt thrown at you - I admire tremendously. Thank you for what you are! God bless you.

Maximilian Schell
P.S. "One can only see good with the heart. The essential is invisible to the eyes." ("The Little Prince").

Janet was also offering support for Michael, and asking her audiences at each of her concerts to say a prayer for her brother. Janet kicked off her janet. world tour. on November 24 in Cincinnati. Following her medley of hits after first hitting the stage, she spoke to her audience, "to ask something of you. Would you please bow your heads and say a silent prayer for my brother, Michael". She continued to ask the audiences in each city on the tour to pray for Michael.

Early in her tour dates had to be canceled it was said due to the flu, but others speculated it may have been due to the tremendous stress she felt in regard to her brother's problems. She later said in an interview that she had to quit watching the news because the things they said about her brother were so upsetting and "just a bunch of B.S."

A special commemorating the twentieth anniversary of the American Music Awards was broadcast on November 27, with a look back at past winners and performers. Michael Jackson was included many times in the review of past years including his show opening performance of "Dangerous" on the 1993 American Music Awards and his joining with other members of USA for Africa on stage to sing "We Are The World" at the finale of the 1986 show. A clip from 1975 has sixteen year old Michael Jackson with a huge afro, dressed in a tuxedo with silver lapels, introducing a "beautiful, talented and charming young lady, my sister Janet Jackson."

Off The Wall magazine, published in England and devoted entirely to Michael Jackson, continued plans as usual for their annual "Michael Jackson Day" in London which was held on November 27. The magazine's editor, Adrian Grant, continued publication of the magazine, offering support for Michael and offering ways in which the fans could show their support.

There were even magazines published that actually focused on Michael's incredible talent, unmatched success, and humanitarianism. The November/December 1993 issue of *Black Beat* magazine was devoted entirely to Michael Jackson and the Jackson family. The collector's issue was filled with stories about Michael and pictures from throughout his career. One article, "Michael Jackson: The Truth" by Carlos Cubas is an interview with Steve Manning, who has known the Jacksons since they were first signed with Motown Records. Manning was the president of the Jackson Five Fan Club and later worked as a publicist for the family. In the interview Manning spoke of Michael's shrewd business sense and his belief in Michael's innocence:

Do you honestly think that he would let what amounts to public child molestation become known? I do believe that Michael is an honest, caring human being, who knows that he has done nothing wrong and is continuing to live his life without fear...If people saw Michael displaying affection towards these kids, it would be very easy to distort the facts and paint a very different picture of actual situations.

Q-ME, Quality - Music & Entertainment maga-zine, in its premiere issue of Winter 1993, featured Michael Jackson on its cover and invited readers to send a message to Michael. Letters written to Michael and sent to the magazine would be forwarded to Michael with some of the letters being published in the maga-zine. An article titled, "A Holiday and New Years Wish for Michael: Leave Him Alone" wondered how Michael would weather the scandal and said that his countless efforts to aid the under-privileged now seemed "over-shadowed by the continuing drama that has plagued his life since late August of this year." The article seemed to waiver back and forth without ever really saying anything though it did concede "Some members of the press feel that celebrities should not receive any special treatment, but I hope in this case celebrity isn't receiving special abuse." The article concluded with a listing of the charities and organizations Michael has contributed to or established in addition to the Heal the World Foundation: Ronald McDonald for Camp Good Times, The Make A Wish Foundation, T.J. Martell Foundation for Leukemia & Cancer Research, United Negro College Fund, The Starlight Foundation, USA for Africa, and Brotman Memorial Burn Center. A second article in the issue, "The Truth About Michael's Drive To Heal The World" outlined Michael's devotion of time, money and love to his Heal the World Foundation. Information on how to contribute or volunteer was also given along with a listing of the organizations, domestic and international, that have collaborated with the Heal the World Foundation in various projects.

On November 26, the Los Angeles Police Depart-ment raided the offices of Michael Jackson's dermatolo-gist, Dr. Arnold Klein, and his plastic surgeon, Dr. Steve

Hoefflin. They hoped to compare information, or photos, contained in the files with the description of Michael's body Jordy had given to police. They confiscated Michael's medical records but did not reveal what they contained. But apparently they did not contain the information they were looking for as a warrant for a body search was obtained for Michael Jackson.

As unscrupulous as the tabloids are in America, they are, unbelievably, even worse in England. Continuing to manufacture stories involving Michael Jackson throughout the entire ordeal, the *London Daily Express* printed an article on November 26, which pretended to be an interview with Jermaine Jackson. In the imaginary chat with the newspaper, Jermaine supposedly said he questioned his brother's innocence. Actually, Jermaine had never spoken to the tabloid and was furious over the article, threatening to sue them for $200 million. Jermaine had consistently stood by Michael's side, defending him and offering support.

Thus far, Pepsi had turned on Michael but Sony's support seemed genuine and unwavering. In late November, a spokesman for Walt Disney World in Orlando, Florida, said Michael Jackson's 3-D movie, *Captain EO* "continues to be one of our most popular attractions." There was said to be no plans to replace the attraction. Sadly, Disney's commitment turned out to be every bit as strong as Pepsi's.

Milking the situation for everything it was worth, *People* magazine featured Michael Jackson on its November 29, 1993 cover with the headline, "Michael Jackson Cracks Up". The accompanying article was merely a rehash of recent events and offered no new information. The majority of the public's responses to this cover story condemned the publication's handling of the story. Readers blasted the magazine for trying and convicting Michael within their pages.

Finally getting sick of the media assassination of her son, Katherine Jackson, with Jermaine, appeared on CNN's *Showbiz Today* and even *Hard Copy* on December 2, to defend Michael. The family had apparently been advised by Michael's representatives to remain quiet about the allegations publicly. Katherine couldn't watch her son be treated so unfairly any longer. "They were telling us not to say anything, but I'm sorry, I'm his mother, I can't sit still and watch them crucify my son and not say anything." Katherine went on to discredit the former security guards refuting each of their claims one by one. Raul Velasco, another former security guard, appeared with Katherine and Jermaine on *Hard Copy*, and noted that he too had been in Michael's private bathroom, and there was never any photo of any nude boy in the room.

Jermaine added, "They found the one thing that he loves to try to bring him down with and that's being around children." He added that his brother is not the weakling many think he is and he will fight, "He's very strong and he's ready to kick some butt."

Both Katherine and Jermaine expressed anger at not being told by Michael's representatives exactly where Michael was staying. Katherine had spoken with Michael on the phone, but she did not know his exact location. Michael had asked his mother about her health, and told her not to worry about him.

There is an interesting note about the interview with Jermaine and Katherine Jackson for *Hard Copy*. All other interviews on the program with people making inflammatory accusations about Michael; the guards, the maid, and later his executive secretary and another security guard, all talked to Diane Dimond, the correspondent heading the show's coverage of the story; but Katherine and Jermaine Jackson talked with Barry Nolan. Perhaps Dimond was not interested in conducting an interview that would be in support of Michael Jackson. Or perhaps Katherine refused to talk with Dimond.

While some of his supposedly closest friends were being conspicuously silent, Michael was getting renewed support from friends Paul McCartney and Stevie Wonder. Even though McCartney and Michael have often disagreed on how best to administer the copyrights in the Beatle catalog, McCartney defended Michael in an interview with an Argentine newspaper, *Clarin*, "Linda and I are parents, and it's clear to us that Michael is not that kind of person." Stevie Wonder told *USA Today*, "I don't believe the allegations. It seems to me, it's almost like a witch hunt because you have these things happening with Michael Jordan, Mike Tyson... It's like people build people up to destroy them. It's very sad. I'm there for him and I always will be." (Wonder's comments seem to be aimed at the media's apparent delight in tearing down the most popular and successful stars, and not that the attacks are necessarily aimed only at people named Michael!)

Michael wasn't getting that kind of support from long time family friend Ben Brown. Brown had known the Jacksons in Gary, Indiana and had worked with them at Steeltown Records. He later worked with Joe Jackson at his now defunct Jackson Records. He had also helped run the home recording studio at Hayvenhurst. Brown was interviewed by *A Current Affair*, and what exactly his position was in regards to the allegations remained foggy at best. If he intended to support Michael, he did about as good a job as LaToya:

> *My personal feelings are that Michael Jackson would not do anything to hurt a child... For me to sit her and say 'No, he's not capable of doing it', I can't say it. For me to say 'I believe he did it', I wouldn't say. However I would say this, I'm concerned about what I am hearing.*
>
> *I just saw Michael spending time with the children. I saw him with them, I saw him carrying them, I saw him just basically spending a lot of time with the children, with the boys and the girls and the children in general. To be as blunt as I can be, I thought he should change that and I was going to advise him of that.*

Later Brown's reason for being on television was made clear when he began promoting his new book on the Jacksons.

Diana Ross talked to Michael on the phone and offered him advice, to come home and face the allegations being made against him, "He must come home and make a stand... Anybody who's accused of wrongdoing needs to." While she may have been offering him advice privately, publicly her silence on the matter was deafening. One of the most asked questions throughout this ordeal was "Where's Diana?".

On December 3, a source was telling the press that Michael Jackson had checked into the Silver Hill Hospital in New Canaan, Connecticut on November 29. Michael's publicist, Lee Solters, denied the story. Columnist Liz Smith wrote that a well connected source told her that Michael was in London, but not at the Charter Clinic as was widely believed, but at a friend's house. There had been a few rumblings in the press that Michael Jackson had visited Elton John's house in London. Some speculated he may be staying there.

In the midst of this mess, the copyright suit against Michael Jackson, Lionel Richie, Quincy Jones, Rod Temperton, and Joseph Jackson went to court on December 7. Reynaud Jones and Robert Smith claimed they had given a demo tape to Joe Jackson in 1977 from which three songs were stolen, "Thriller", "The Girl is Mine", and "We Are The World". Reynaud Jones said he also considered suing Michael Jackson over "Billie Jean".

During the proceedings five hours of Michael's testimony, taped in Mexico City, was finally played giving the public their first sense of his condition upon canceling the Dangerous tour. After weeks of skepticism surrounding his statement of his painkiller dependency, the public could finally see for themselves. Michael was obviously under the influence of some type of medication. He appeared very drowsy, barely able to concentrate throughout the deposition. Though he did answer all of the questions, he had difficulty at times understanding the questions put before him, often asking that the questions be repeated. Asked to spell his last name for the record, he spells out Jackson very, very slowly. At one point he even struggles to name all the members of the Jackson 5, counting on his fingers to make sure he included everyone. (Actually, he got it wrong, he included Randy who wasn't a member of the Jackson 5, only the Jacksons.) The questioning is even stopped at one point so Michael can take a break as he is suffering pain in his mouth due to his recent oral surgery. When the questioning resumes, he admits he did take a painkiller during the break.

In his taped testimony, Michael said, "I wouldn't cheat anybody out of any credit. I am an honest person." He adds, "Any songs that I take credit for on my album, any songs that say Michael Jackson, are written by me...I'm a songwriter myself. I write my own songs. I don't have to take other people songs." He described how ideas for songs come to him saying, "I'm just a source through which they come. It's a beautiful thing. It's very spiritual. It's like standing under a tree and letting a leaf fall and trying to catch it. It's that beautiful."

He also described how he came to be involved with the USA for Africa project, with Quincy Jones asking him to write the song and appealing to his love for children. Michael refused at first saying, "I just finished *Thriller*, I spent all that time in the studio. But he said it would be very important for the children. As soon as he said that, he knows how I feel about children."

Small portions of his taped testimony were broadcast on newscasts and scandal shows showing Michael's condition when he was forced to cancel his tour. *A Current Affair* showed a portion of the tape then asked viewers to take part in a phone poll asking whether or not they felt Michael was really addicted to the painkillers. In their usual uncolored, totally unbiased, language they asked what viewers thought of "that performance for the camera". Overwhelmingly, the viewers thought the tape did prove Michael was in fact addicted to the painkillers, 68.71% of the callers answered yes, he was addicted, while 31.29% answered no, he was not addicted.

As music stars gathered for the Billboard Awards on December 8, Michael Jackson was predictably a hot topic of conversation. Queen Latifah said angrily that the attack on Michael "is bullshit. He's innocent until proven guilty." She referred to LaToya as "a basketcase." Teddy Riley said, "Michael's coming back. As a friend I say to him, 'We're all behind you'." Quincy Jones added, "It's awful the way things have been exaggerated. He's been indicted before he's had a chance to say anything."

The Conspiracy Tapes, which aired on December 8, took a look at different stories and compared the official view of events up against the conspiratorial view. This particular show looked at the Michael Jackson story with different views offered by Anthony Pellicano, Brett Barnes, Wade Robson, and J. Randy Taraborrelli being compared to claims made by the dentist, Ernie Rizzo, Gloria Allred, and Larry Feldman.

A tape of Chandler talking with his son's stepfather has Chandler threatening, "I will humiliate him beyond belief if I don't get want I want." Rizzo submits here that Chandler obviously wants his son, and points out that there is no mention of money on this tape. That is not obvious to anyone else, and where does he ever mention his son?

A taped phone conversation between Pellicano and Chandler's first lawyer, Barry Rothman, has them discussing movie deals with Rothman refusing to mention any number of movie deals or amounts of money. Pellicano asks Rothman, "Convince me that it would be better for me to give him more than one deal. Convince me." Rothman replies, "That's a given." Pellicano: "There's no given there." Rothman: "I don't have to state the obvious and I'm not prepared to do so in this conversation."

Larry Feldman, responding to Michael's announcement that he was seeking treatment for a dependency on painkillers, said, "I have no information on whether he's a drug addict or not. But it's pretty outrageous for him to try to relate it, if he is a drug addict, to relate it to this little thirteen year old boy causing him to be a drug addict. This is unbelievable." What is truly outrageous is that Feldman may actually believe this statement. Why would Michael Jackson feel any stress in his life at this time? Certainly the allegation itself and the media's lynching of him, and its potential ruining of his career and his life are nothing to worry about.

LaToya, in another sudden change of heart about Michael, held a press conference at midnight on December 8 in Tel Aviv, Israel, to announce, "Michael is my brother and I love him a great deal. But, I cannot and will not be a silent collaborator of his crimes against small innocent children... I love my brother but it's wrong. I don't want to see these kids hurt." She claimed further that her mother had shown her checks Michael had written made payable to the parents of children "for large sums", and that the rest of the family defended Michael because he supports them financially and they feared he would cut off the money if they didn't. LaToya added that her mother would refer to Michael as "that damn faggot".

LaToya's husband/manager Jack Gordon, never at a loss for outrageous tales to tell, told the press that Michael had threatened to kill LaToya and tried to kidnap her twice to keep her silent! While this is of course ludicrous, LaToya did receive death threats from fans of Michael's.

The Jackson family, including Katherine, Joseph, Jackie, Tito, Jermaine, and Randy, immediately held a live press conference in front of Hayvenhurst to refute LaToya's most unbelievable, yet most inflammatory, claims to date. The impromptu interview was carried live by CNN. During the interview by CNN reporter Jim Moret Katherine denied ever showing any checks to LaToya and ever making the remarks about Michael that LaToya said she did. In fact, Katherine has long fought any accusations about Michael's sexuality. Katherine angrily charged that LaToya was making these claims so she too could profit from selling her story to tabloids and talk shows. Joseph said, "We hope Michael's fans all over the world won't believe this." Jermaine answered LaToya's remarks saying, "There is no validity to what she is saying. It is absolutely not true. My brother is not a child molester."

It would seem Katherine was right, LaToya and Jack Gordon would soon be making the rounds of all the talk shows. The very next day Sybil, rather LaToya, told the *Today Show*, "I have never, ever, seen Michael in bed with another boy."

Later LaToya made another appearance on *Geraldo* where she said she believed Michael was guilty because he frequently had young boys visit with him at the house in Encino. She admitted she never saw her brother act improperly toward any boy, but believes he is guilty anyway.

Attempting to cast doubt on other of Michael's comments, LaToya told Geraldo she was not aware of any skin disorder in the family and that Michael had a prescription for a skin cream in the name of a security person. Miko Brando would pick up the order. Actually vitiligo does run in the Jackson family, on Joseph's side. Also, Janet was the only family member that knew Michael had vitiligo. She swore to Michael she would never tell, and she never did.

Joseph and Katherine Jackson agreed to appear on *Geraldo* to refute LaToya's comments. They then thought better of it and canceled their appearance.

Jack Gordon said LaToya chose her time in Israel to launch her bombshell against her brother because it is the Holy Land and you should tell the truth. Obviously they feel very differently about other parts of the world as their stories seemed to change so drastically, it's very difficult to tell which emotional tell all interview is the truth.

Comedian Dennis Miller had his first time on world wide television when he hosted a segment on CNN on December 10. He said he debated about what to say to people half way around the world and settled on, "LaToya - Shut Up!!!", no doubt echoing many people's thoughts exactly.

LaToya talked with Maury Povich by telephone from Tel Aviv for one of his shows focusing on Michael. Leroy Thomas and Fred Hammond also appeared on *Maury Povich* and while still claiming they were fired for knowing too much, they said they saw many kids visit the Encino home, they stated they didn't think this was unusual, and they specifically stated they never saw Michael Jackson molest any child. They also described some situations they felt were questionable, such as Michael phoning the house to see who was home before he came to the house, and his asking the guards to hold a child in the guard house until he called for him, and of course the alleged nude photo Thomas was ordered to destroy. During the program, Thomas offered to take a lie detector test, saying if he failed, he would drop the lawsuit. Povich would later take him up on his offer.

A phone conversation between Maury Povich and LaToya, taped earlier from Tel Aviv had LaToya saying she never saw Michael in bed with any boy, but she believed her brother was guilty. She stated she saw a check in the amount of $1 million made out to the father of a young boy. She also stated she didn't believe Michael was really addicted to drugs, that it was a made up story.

Joseph and Katherine Jackson, who were contacted by phone for the program, refuted the claims made by the guards and by LaToya. Katherine insisted she never saw any checks in Michael's room and certainly never called her son a faggot.

Raul Velasco, who also worked as a security guard at Hayvenhurst the same time as Thomas and Hammond, told Povich there was no improper behavior with Michael and any young boys. A bodyguard seated in the audience, who had worked for the Jacksons for fifteen years, told Povich he didn't know how Thomas and Hammond could make these allegations. Jackson family friend Majestik Magnificent also defended Michael. As did Tatiana Thumbtzen, who co-starred with Michael in the video for "The Way You Make Me Feel". She revealed her friendship with Michael blossomed into a year long love affair, refusing to reveal how intimate they became. She called the allegations ridiculous and was amazed at how far the whole thing had gone.

Leroy Thomas appeared once again on *Maury Povich* after he did submit to a polygraph test. The results showed he was truthful on some questions, but he failed other questions, most notably that Michael had asked him to destroy a photo of a nude boy. His reason for continuing to make these claims became clear when he went on to announce on the show that he is currently working on a book about Michael Jackson. There is no doubt Michael's legions of fans will avidly avoid this and similar efforts sure to result from the ongoing persecution of Michael Jackson.

5

"Don't treat me like a criminal"

Friday, December 10, Michael Jackson once again proved all the rumor-mongers and skeptics wrong when he did in fact return home to the United States. He arrived, after a stop in Billings, Montana, at Santa Barbara airport in a private 747 jet. He was accompanied by two young friends, two brothers from New Jersey, Eddie and Frank Cascio ages nine and thirteen. He disembarked, dressed in a red hat and shirt, and was immediately whisked away in a white van.

Johnnie Cochran, Michael's newly appointed attorney, told the press, "He's back and he's determined to establish his innocence." Camera crews, photographers and reporters immediately staked out the ranch waiting for a glimpse of Michael, or any tidbit of information. The departure of a chimp in a truck, the delivery of an arcade sized video game, and the discovery of two fans who had made their way on to the property all made the news. *A Current Affair* rented a helicopter and hovered above the ranch, noting that some rides were on in the amusement park and reporting very seriously that Michael was "staying inside"!

Michael's return was said to be on the condition that any body search be conducted with confidentiality and discretion, and that there weren't any secret arrest warrants or indictments waiting for him.

USA Today reporter Marco R. della Cava, in compiling a story on the Michael Jackson case, was contacted by a man who represented dancer Eddie Reynoza. He said Reynoza, who had earlier told *A Current Affair*, "I'm not asking for a penny and I never will ask for a penny", would play his tape of his phone conversation with Michael Jackson from November 18 in which Michael supposedly tells Reynoza he is not coming back to the United States. A meeting was set up with Reynoza then canceled when Mr. "I never will ask for a penny" Reynoza found out the paper does not pay for interviews. The credibility of the tape was further hampered by the fact that Michael Jackson was already home!

The December 11, 1993, issue of *Billboard* magazine celebrated twenty five years of music and entertainment for concert promoter Marcel Avram. A special section devoted to Avram was comprised of the usual congratulatory ads placed by friends and associates. A completely dark page with only a picture of Michael's eyes read, "Marcel, Congratulations on 25 years. Love, Michael Jackson." One ad was different from the rest. Instead of congratulating the person being recognized in the issue, it was placed by Marcel

Avram. The ad featured a color photo of Michael Jackson in concert that spanned two pages and read:

Dangerous World Tour 1993/94
Michael Jackson Produced by Marcel Avram Mama
Concerts & Rau

It was accompanied by a listing of sold out concert dates and a note to Michael:

Michael, get well soon and hopefully we'll see you back on stage in the near future!

Thanks to S. Gallin, J. Morey, B. Fields, S. Chabre, B. Bray, B. Grey, H. Sinclare, N. Dugdale and everyone involved for making the biggest and most successful world tour that has ever been staged.

Due to the media's massacre of the Michael Jackson story, airplay of his music was stopped by radio station KEZK-FM in St. Louis. The station's operations manager and the general manager made the decision that it was "inappropriate to feature this artist given the holiday focus on children." On December 14, the station began airing an editorial voiced by the operations manager, Robert Burch, stating that they in no way wished to assess the guilt or innocence of Michael Jackson and acknowledged Michael's contributions of money, time, and energy on behalf of children.

Robert Burch said the decision was in part because of the seemingly unending media coverage of the molestation allegations against Michael Jackson. "You couldn't turn on the TV or pick up a newspaper without hearing about it". Burch also pointed out that at this time the community was disturbed by the fact that children in St. Louis had been the victim of a series of unsolved murders and a serial killer was suspected. Being the holidays, the station felt Michael Jackson's music was inappropriate for their family oriented image.

It wasn't explained how or why a suspected serial killer in St. Louis was being connected with playing Michael Jackson's music or how Michael's music had changed to now be considered "inappropriate". Up until then, his music was considered very appropriate. How had his music changed? Although in their editorial they claimed they did not wish to assess his guilt or innocence, that certainly wasn't the result. It seemed as though they were ignoring some very significant facts: like a person is supposed to be presumed innocent until proven guilty by a court of law, not a radio station, and therefore should not be punished; that there was no evidence to suggest Michael was guilty of anything; and there were no charges against him. The station did make the very generous concession that when Michael's problems were solved, they would *consider* adding his music back to their play list.

In response to the station's decision, the general manager reportedly received angry phone calls from managers of other radio stations in the area. A local top forty station took the situation in a humorous fashion, announcing they would begin an all Amy Grant format!

Actually the station's decision to drop Michael Jackson from their playlist is much less surprising and less poignant after learning they are known for shying away from any controversy at all. The station had earlier dropped Madonna's music from their playlist after her controversial book, *Sex*, was published. Her music has not been added back since.

Six members of the Jackson family joined together again for a live interview on BET on December 14 to defend Michael and to express their determination not to let this bring them down. The interview was live from their Encino home. Katherine told BET, "It's just allegations. They're trying my son before he's even accused." Jermaine added, "We will not buckle. We will not bow down to what's being said."

One week after his return home, *Hard Copy* reported Michael Jackson was selling his beloved Neverland Valley Ranch. They showed the ad that was to run in the weekend's paper listing the property for $22 million. Later Beverly Hills realtor Mike Silverman said Neverland was not for sale, it had been confused with a nearby ranch. *Hard Copy* did admit their error saying they were told the property was Michael Jackson's. It does leave a question of how thorough the program is in digging up information however, and how well it is verified, if at all. It supports further the idea that these shows only look for someone to say something is true, whether or not it actually is true is immaterial.

On December 13, Michael's lawyers were in court asking that a gag order be placed on the proceedings in the civil case. They asked that information connected with the civil case not be shared with investigators or the media. Their request was denied by Judge Rothman on December 17. Even though the judge admitted the case had already received an incredible amount of publicity, he ruled against the order that would have prevented the lawyers from discussing with the media any information learned during the discovery process. However, both sides did agree to guidelines with regards to the media. They agreed not to identify the boy or to release any medical records.

After returning home, Michael took more control over his defense and made some changes in his defense team. Pellicano and Fields were now off the case. While some reports said they were fired, Pellicano told *USA Today* that it was his decision to leave, that he had done all he could do. He added his departure should not be attributed to the merits of the case and that he firmly believes in Michael's innocence. Fields was reported to have been replaced because of his blunder in court in November when he told a judge, and therefore the media and the whole world, that they expected an indictment very soon.

Behind the scenes, the situation was very unorganized. The attorneys, each representing a different firm, weren't really a team. Each was fighting for control, being aware that there was a lot of money and prestige at stake along with possible control of the legal matters in connection with his musical empire. Michael's manager, Sandy Gallin, told *The Wall Street Journal* that "When Michael was away and unreachable, there really wasn't anybody in control."

On December 3 a letter, signed by Michael, was sent to Fields ousting him as chief of the civil case. On the 13th, he resigned under pressure. John Branca, the attorney who represented Michael throughout the eighties and helped negotiate his deal to purchase the Beatle catalog, was also exercising some influence in the decision to replace Fields.

Attorney Johnnie Cochran Jr. then joined Michael's defense team with Howard Weitzman. Cochran told *Jet* magazine, "I'm really pleased to be representing Mr. Jackson. I expect he will be totally vindicated.

Their charges are false. He is innocent and it is outrageous the way he has been treated by the media. A lot of people will owe him an apology when it's over."

Katherine Jackson, who had publicly criticized Michael's defense team said with the changes, she could sleep better at night. Some in the media speculated that the family had had some influence on Michael's decision to make the changes. This seems unlikely. Although Michael is very close to his mother, it is doubtful he would let her influence such a critical decision. He has never been one to agree with his family's advice. It does seem plausible that another lady in his life would have such influence, Elizabeth Taylor. In fact, her attorney, Neil Papiano, was also brought in to monitor the case. Field's replacement, Cochran, was actually suggested by Bob Jones. Jones had known Cochran since they went to high school together.

Rumors were now running rampant that Michael would attend the wedding of Donald Trump and Marla Maples at the Plaza Hotel in New York. He did not attend.

Shannon Reeves, the West Coast Region Director of the National Association for the Advancement of Colored People called a news conference for Monday, December 20, to discuss, "the media bashing of entertainer Michael Jackson and to address how other economically powerful African Americans have been victimized by the press."

The coverage of the allegations facing Michael Jackson is excessive. You have made the point. There have been no charges filed. If there are charges filed in the Jackson case, those charges will be filed in the courtroom, not the newsroom. If there is to be someone to judge the case it will not be the evening news anchor, it will be someone who is elected or party to the bench. If there is someone to hear the facts in the case and make a decision, it will not be the news pool or editorial room or editorial board, it will be a jury of his peers.

With his health much improved, Michael really took control, took to his own defense and launched an offense. "Demonstrating media power normally reserved for world leaders", Michael Jackson issued a long awaited statement which was carried live on CNN, E!, and MTV on December 22, 1993 at 3:00 P.M. EST:

"Good afternoon. To all my friends and fans, I wish to convey my deepest gratitude for your love and support. I am doing well and I am strong.

As you may already know, after my tour ended I remained out of the country undergoing treatment for a dependency on pain medication. This medication was initially prescribed to soothe the excruciating pain that I was suffering after recent reconstructive surgery on my scalp.

There have been many disgusting statements made recently concerning allegations of improper conduct on my part. These statements about me are totally false. As I have maintained from the very beginning, I am hoping for a speedy end to this horrifying, horrifying experience to which I have been subjected.

I shall not in this statement respond to all the false allegations being made against me, since my lawyers have advised me that this is not the proper forum in which to do that. I will say I am particularly upset by the handling of this mass matter by the incredible, terrible mass media. At every opportunity, the media has dissected and manipulated these allegations to reach their own conclusions. I ask all of you to wait to hear the truth before you label or condemn me. Don't treat me like a criminal, because I am innocent.

I have been forced to submit to a dehumanizing and humiliating examination by the Santa Barbara County Sheriff's Department and the Los Angeles Police Department earlier this week. They served a search warrant on me which allowed them to view and photograph my body, including my penis, my buttocks, my lower torso, thighs, and any other areas that they wanted. They were supposedly looking for any discoloration, spotting, blotches or other evidence of a skin color disorder called vitiligo which I have previously spoken about.

The warrant also directed me to cooperate in any examination of my body by their physician to determine the condition of my skin, including whether I have vitiligo or any other skin disorder. The warrant further stated that I had no right to refuse the examination or photographs and if I failed to cooperate with them they would introduce that refusal at any trial as an indication of my guilt.

It was the most humiliating ordeal of my life - one that no person should ever have to suffer. And even after experiencing the indignity of this search, the parties involved were still not satisfied and wanted to take even more pictures. It was a nightmare, a horrifying nightmare. But if this is what I have to endure to prove my innocence, my complete innocence, so be it.

Throughout my life, I have only tried to help thousands upon thousands of children to live happy lives. It brings tears to my eyes when I see any child who suffers.

If I am guilty of anything, it is of believing what God said about children: 'Suffer little children to come unto me and forbid them not, for such is the kingdom of heaven.' In no way do I think that I am God, but I do try to be God-like in my heart.

I am totally innocent of any wrongdoing and I know these terrible allegations will all be proven false. Again, to my friends and fans, thank you very much for all of your support. Together we will see this through to the very end. I love you very much and may God bless you all. I love you. Goodbye.

The entire statement was aired later by *Hard Copy* with responses from the public which were overwhelmingly supportive of Michael Jackson. *A Current Affair* also carried the entire statement with trial lawyer Barry Slotnick reviewing it, saying it was a long time in coming, that Michael's advisors were correct in having Michael tell his side of the story. The same show later hired a voice analyst to do an "expert analysis" of Michael's statement. He reviewed the statement and found him to be lying, he found that Michael himself didn't believe what he was saying! It would be interesting to see what this "expert" would find if he reviewed some of the outrageous statements made by the hosts and reporters on this show.

The E! Entertainment Network had carried the statement live and later rebroadcast it during their entertainment news program. Those shows and newscasts that didn't air the entire statement, aired clip after clip of Michael declaring his innocence, "Don't treat me like a criminal because I am innocent."

The same day that Michael took to the airwaves, his attorney's, Howard Weitzman and Johnnie Cochran, were guests on *Larry King Live*. Weitzman told King:

What Johnnie and I tried to do here, it was really Michael's idea and Michael's statement, was level the playing field. The way this thing has been covered, it has not been fair, it has not been fair to Michael. It was important to Michael, and Johnnie and I agreed, that he let the public know he's back, he's strong, he's innocent, he didn't do it and what he's going through, gone through, and willing to go through to prove his innocence.

Weitzman brought up the possibility that the boy had been put up to making the allegations and at one point had recanted his allegations to investigators.

Public reaction to his statement was strong. Polls conducted by various TV shows and publications showed a dramatic increase in the number of people who believed Michael Jackson. Despite *A Current Affair's* efforts to discredit Michael's statements, their follow up poll showed a huge increase in the percentage of people who believed Michael Jackson, 73.73% said they believed Michael Jackson while 26.27% said they believed the allegations were true. It was exactly what the public was waiting for, for Michael Jackson to publicly declare his innocence. The statement made top story news on the networks and was front page news the next morning. Several magazines also carried segments of the statement, *Jet* magazine carried a complete printed copy of Michael's statement along with an interview with Joseph and Katherine who defended Michael and said they didn't know why LaToya was making the statements she had made.

The Jackson family issued a statement to the media following Michael's live address, " The Jackson family has always and will continue to stand by Michael.

We believe in his innocence and are confident that his dignity and humanity will prevail."

Los Angeles authorities scheduled a press conference in response to Michael's public address. It was later canceled.

The day following the statement by Michael, his attorneys Howard Weitzman and Johnnie Cochran appeared on *Today* where they revealed that hundreds of people had been questioned in connection with the case and almost without exception they said they were treated always appropriately, and that Michael never did anything improper. Weitzman said "The problem is Michael Jackson has been tried and crucified on innuendo and speculation and no facts." He added that witnesses, under oath, said *Hard Copy* lied to them and tricked them.

While Michael Jackson was in seclusion receiving treatment for his addiction, Larry Feldman implied that if Michael Jackson were innocent, he would come home, face his accusers and declare his innocence. When Michael regained his health, returned home and took the offensive against the allegations and the media, Feldman accused Michael of trying the case in the press and grandstanding! Feldman also accused Michael and his attorneys of purposely scheduling the statement while he was out of town.

Fans in Washington, D.C. brightened Michael's holidays by sending him a seven foot card wishing him the best for the holidays and a joyous new year. The goal, according to Fred Outten, the organizer of the project, was to recognize Michael Jackson, "not only as the world's greatest entertainer, but also for his lifetime humanitarian contributions to society."

Time magazine's pick for the Man of the Year was announced on Christmas. Before the unveiling, the Vice President and Executive Producer for *CNN Special Reports*, hinted that the Man of the Year was plural and may be the two Michael's - Jackson and Jordan. Earlier in the year basketball great Michael Jordan had surprisingly retired from the NBA following allegations against him that he was a compulsive gambler and following the murder of his father. The Man of the Year was plural, but not Jackson and Jordan. It was four peacemakers involved in the Mid East peace plan.

People magazine's year end issue listed their choices for "The 25 Most Intriguing People of the Year", which included Michael Jackson. The review of the "Best of Tube" for the year included *Michael Jackson Talks to...Oprah*, which was described as the TV mega-event of the year.

Billboard's year end issue counted down the top artists, singles and albums in several categories with Michael making a strong showing considering his album was released more than two years earlier and he spent the latter part of the year buried by scandal, rumors, and lies:

Top Pop Artists: #34 Michael Jackson
Top Billboard 200 Album Artists: #41 Michael Jackson
Top Billboard 200 Album: #38 *Dangerous*
Top Billboard 200 Album Artists - Male: #16 Michael Jackson
Top Pop Catalog Albums: #31 *Thriller*
Hot 100 Singles Artists: #17 Michael Jackson
Hot 100 Singles: #47 "Will You Be There"
Hot 100 Singles Artists - Male: #4 Michael Jackson
Hot 100 Singles Sales: #60 "Will You Be There"

Hot 100 Singles Airplay: #35 "Will You Be There"
Top R&B Album Artists: #30 Michael Jackson
Top R&B Albums: #28 *Dangerous*
Hot R&B Singles: #88 "Who Is It"
Top R&B Artists: #34 Michael Jackson
Hot R&B Singles Airplay: #69 "Who Is It"
Hot Adult Contemporary Artists: #12 Michael Jackson
Hot Adult Contemporary Singles and Tracks: #26 "Will
You Be There", #35 "Heal the World"
Hot Dance Music Club Play Singles: #50 "Who Is It"
Hot Dance Music Maxi Singles Sales: #40 "Who Is It"

   In a review of the year in music, the publication focused solely on Michael's music, "given that virtually no nugget of information has gone unexamined, we don't feel any real need to explore it here. On a business front, sales of Jackson's albums haven't diminished, according to retailers, ..."
   Michael's previous albums continued to sell strong. Eleven years after its release, *Thriller* had sold another one million copies in the U.S. during the year, bringing the U.S. sales to 22 million copies, remaining the best selling album in the United States. Worldwide sales of *Thriller* now topped 50 million, with it remaining the world's biggest selling album in history. It was no longer the biggest selling foreign album in Japan however-er. The soundtrack album for *The Bodyguard* had sales in Japan of 1.8 million copies, topping *Thriller's* Japanese sales of 1.6 million copies.
   Michael Jackson's Dangerous tour was reported to be the number one grossing concert tour of North America of 1993. With only five concerts in Mexico City, the Dangerous tour, which *A Current Affair* had declared as being jeopardized, had grossed $12.5 million.

At the end of December, Michael's attorneys were in court in response to reports that the photographs taken of Michael during the body search were being leaked to the press. Cochran and Weitzman were seeking to insure the security of the photographs and block their possible sale. Feldman, a few days later, filed court documents in an effort to obtain the photos of Michael taken during the body search.

Back 2 Back, a rap duo comprised of twin ten year old boys from Bowling Green, Virginia, released their debut single at year end, "Michael". The lyrics are in support of their idol:

> *You have done so much for us children*
> *And Michael you help us when we need you*
> *What else could we do but stand by you*
> *When you need us*

James and Jeremy Alsop decided to compose and sing the song to Michael in lieu of writing him a letter. Their mother, Anita Alsop, said she had discussed Michael's situation with them, "I watched it, I've read it, "I've explained it to the children. It's all false. I think it's a money making scheme. Michael is as innocent as I'm James and Jeremy's mother. And that's how they feel about it too."

Meanwhile, legal problems continued to mount for Michael. On December 28, 1993, concert promoter Marcel Avram filed a breach of contract complaint in Los Angeles Superior Court against Michael Jackson, TTC Touring Corp., and MJJ Enterprises. The suit, asking for $20 million in damages plus punitive damages, charged fraud, negligent misrepresentation, and breach of fiduciary duty regarding Michael's contract with

Avram's Mama Concerts to finance and promote the 1993 Dangerous World Tour. Avram and Pebbles Music Inc., co-plaintiffs in the case, alleged Michael Jackson concealed the true facts regarding his condition and actions upon signing the contract. The concert promoter claimed Michael's performances on the tour "...were not first class as guaranteed by the contract but, instead, were mediocre, abbreviated, and mechanical as compared with his prior performances." Nineteen of the forty three scheduled dates were canceled when the tour was ended in November.

MJJ Enterprises president Stephen Chabre had engaged in settlement negotiations with the tour promoter since the end of the tour in an attempt to solve it amicably. Lloyds of London had provided $20 million of insurance to the promoters. Lloyds' spokesman, Matt Huber, commented that if the promoters had a valid claim, that the tour was canceled due to Michael Jackson's drug addiction, the claim would be paid.

The Children's Peace Foundation was also jumping on the sue Michael Jackson bandwagon, suing him for breach of contract, fraud, negligent misrepresentation and unfair competition. The foundation claimed Michael Jackson used them to make lucrative merchandising deals and then cut them out of the profits.

Rumors continued to be made up and spread faster than wildfire. The latest now was that Michael Jackson had paid Brooke Shields to be his date at public engagements and that they later grew to be genuine friends. Michael was rumored to have paid Shields $10,000 per appearance.

Plans to begin re-marketing Michael's fragrances, Mystique de Michael Jackson for women and Legende de Michael Jackson for men, were canceled in December. The makers of the line said it was due to Michael's addiction to painkillers. The cologne was sold through The Michael Jackson International Fan Club and through television ads only.

Feldman filed a motion in Superior Court on December 30, to compel Michael to answer a list of questions for the civil suit. The over one hundred written questions asked for information about each person under the age of eighteen that Michael has entertained since January 1, 1983. With his refusal to supply any of this information, Feldman accused him of stonewalling. Stonewall Jackson had previously only provided the answers to three of the questions, his name, birthdate, and where he lives.

Michael was meanwhile spending the New Year holiday in Las Vegas. He arrived on Thursday, December 30, and was seen visiting the Treasure Island complex recently opened by his friend, Steve Wynn. He was in good spirits and waved to fans. He was also seen with his friend Michael Milken.

New Years Day Michael was the most watchable star attending the much ballyhooed Barbra Streisand concert at the MGM Grand Garden. The audience applauded him as he was escorted to his seat. He attended the show with Michael Milken, and later visited with Streisand backstage. That afternoon Michael reportedly spent two hours at the MGM Grand Hotel's theme park in heavy disguise.

The January issue of *Vanity Fair* claimed to provide "the definitive account of Jackson's fall". The article, "Nightmare In Neverland" by Maureen Orth, gave an account of the whole story from the time Michael first met the boy to the making of the allegations, the filing of the civil suit and the following media explosion. The article was based on information from attorneys and investigators from both sides, but still seemed to give a bit more undue credibility to the boy's side.

In promoting the issue of the magazine, Orth was a guest on *Larry King Live*. She gave a rather detailed overview of the boy's side of the story taken from court documents, but barley mentioned the possible extortion plot, mentioning only that it too is detailed in the article. Little, if any, time on the program was spent on this part of the story.

Also appearing on the program was J. Randy Taraborrelli who noted that generally, many of the so called witnesses are suspect. He noted that *everybody* even remotely connected to this case asked for money to talk. Even Joseph Jackson. Katherine Jackson, who phoned in to the program, denied it, but many sources have revealed that Joseph Jackson offered to give an interview to *Hard Copy*, for $100,000. The deal reportedly fell through because the show wanted both Joseph and Katherine Jackson and Joe couldn't guarantee Katherine's participation.

Taraborrelli reiterated his belief that Michael would indeed return home and face the allegations against him, "I think Michael Jackson is not the wimp that many people believe he is. He's been running a huge corporation, he's been making million of dollars for a long time and you don't get that way by running away from your problems."

A caller to the show made an interesting observation about the young boy accusing Michael Jackson. Taraborrelli had pointed out that Michael was a very successful and shrewd businessman. The caller observed

that the young boy, at age 13, was also a shrewd businessman.

In a following issue of *Vanity Fair*, Roseanne
Arnold spoke of Michael Jackson saying he, "is the
perfect picture of a child molester. He had the perfect
circumstances. He's 35 fucking years old and I think he
got all this facial surgery done to obscure his age." She
didn't explain how having a nose job related to molesting a child. It is probably a safe bet that many child
molesters, who have been actually charged, tried and
convicted, have their original nose. That Michael
Jackson spends time with children does not in any way
prove, or even suggest, he is a child molester.

Vanessa Williams and Harry Connick Jr. hosted
Grammy's Greatest Moments which aired on January 5.
The special look back at previous Grammy Award shows
featured performances and award winners. Included was
an all too brief look at Michael's performance of "Man
in the Mirror" from 1988, the only time he has ever
performed on the award show. Also featured were
quick glimpses of Michael Jackson and Quincy Jones
winning big in 1984, the Grammy victories of USA for
Africa for "We Are The World", and Michael in 1993
proving "me and Janet really are two different people."

Not surprisingly, the NFL had a hard time
coming up with a halftime performer for the Super Bowl
to follow the previous year's extravaganza staged by
Michael Jackson. Country star Garth Brooks was
approached but he turned it down. Brooks was refused
the money he had asked for to stage the kind of production he wanted, "Following Michael Jackson is harder
than anything in the entertainment business, so I wanted
all the gags and gifts. The league came up just a little
short. I didn't feel I had the room to compromise."

Game time came frighteningly near before a halftime show was finally announced, which included a lineup of country performers featuring a one time reunion of the Judds.

Early in January reports began surfacing in the tabloids that a settlement of $10 million was being negotiated to end the civil proceeding and possibly end the criminal investigation. Attorneys for both sides refused to comment on any such negotiations. Later in the month, a London tabloid, *Today*, claimed Michael Jackson's accuser had signed a tentative agreement to end the civil lawsuit for $49 million! An associated report had this rumor being purposely made up by an American tabloid in an attempt to track down a suspected story leak. Most credible sources did confirm that a settlement was being negotiated but not for the astronomical sums being reported. Some sources had Michael paying up to $100 million! *Time* magazine reported that the true figure was closer to $5 million.

Following Michael's live statement and the resulting dramatic swing of public opinion in his favor, Feldman had to somehow even the score. A statement taken from the boy on December 28 was filed in Los Angeles Superior Court on January 10 which detailed, again, the specific acts which the boy said he and Michael engaged in. Howard Weitzman explained the new court document, which contained nothing that hadn't already been detailed in August, was simply a counter punch by Feldman following Michael's very public statement. He very much needed to keep the allegations in the mind of the public, and especially potential jurors, "Because it's clearly this kid's story against Jackson's story. So the motion was really filed to generate more publicity to get out there these allegations to attempt to make Michael look bad so you'll ask me the type of questions you're asking me, and to generate amongst potential jurors a negative image of Michael. That's what that motion was all about." The statement was filed by Feldman as part of a request for Michael's detailed financial records. He figured he would need such information in assessing a proper amount of damages should he actually win the case. One more in a long line of indications that Chandler was very interested in money from the case and nothing more.

Weitzman went on to blast the media coverage:

First, to get fair treatment, I think is almost impossible given the way the media conducts themselves, both video, radio and print today because part of the sales process for the news media is to titillate and excite and of course the going theory is that sex excites.

...I would impose some sanctions on the testimony of someone who was paid. The problem is these people go out without talking with their lawyers, so they have no control in large part over some greedy individual. Like the maid for example who got paid $20,000 or the security guards who got paid $150,000 so they can get on **Hard Copy**, *a program that will do anything to get viewers. The truth is not a criterion for that particular program.*

Quincy Jones also publicly denounced the media in their handling of the story, "The media is dealing with a feeding frenzy. They have overstepped their bounds by 200 miles to indict somebody before he's even tried, or even accused. It's amazing. But, I saw Michael over the holidays and he's holding up, he's strong. He looks good. We've got all our prayers with him."

Michael's manager, Sandy Gallin, who had been criticized by some for being conspicuously silent throughout this ordeal, staunchly defended Michael in an interview with the *Los Angeles Times*. He went on to predict Michael would be exonerated.

Beginning January 11, Michael Jackson's accuser would no longer be referred to by the media as "the thirteen year old boy". Jordy Chandler turned fourteen.

After only three hours of deliberation on January 12, a federal jury decided the songs, "Thriller", "We Are The World", and "The Girl is Mine" are indeed the works of Rod Temperton, Michael Jackson and Lionel Richie, and Michael Jackson respectively, and were not stolen from Reynaud Jones and Robert Smith, the songwriters from Indiana who sued Michael Jackson, et al., for $400 million.

This wasn't the only copyright case going on that Michael was interested in. Michael was among songwriters who filed papers in connection with a copyright infringement case brought against 2 Live Crew. The rap group was being sued for using Roy Orbison's "Pretty Woman" in a song parody. Michael's argument was that the group, or persons making a parody of a song, should be responsible for paying royalties to the song's composer. Michael is not against the art of parody. "Weird Al" Yankovic has parodied Michael's hits "Beat It" and "Bad", put unlike the 2 Live Crew case, Yankovic paid all royalties due Michael for the use of his music.

On January 14, Judge Rothman postponed Michael's deposition, scheduled for January 18, and two hearings. One hearing was to rule on whether Michael would be compelled to answer the written questions submitted by Feldman, the other was to rule on whether Feldman was entitled to the photos of Michael taken during the body search. The hearings were rescheduled for January 25 and Michael was ordered to give his deposition between January 25 and February 1.

It was being reported around this time that Michael had added three new investigators to his team. Michael's attorneys, anxious to have the criminal investigation completed before the civil trial began, said that Michael may not show up for his scheduled deposition unless the criminal investigation was completed.

Also working diligently on the case was *Hard Copy*. They had now dug up *another* former employee of Michael Jackson's to do one of their ever so lucrative "exclusive" interviews. Orietta Murdoch had worked as Michael's executive secretary for two years, leaving in 1991. She had quit, not because of any concerns over Michael's behavior, but because she was refused a pay increase. The former secretary admitted to Diane Dimond that she never witnessed any improper behavior but did see many kids spending time with Michael Jackson. About the only thing that was learned in the multi part interview about Michael Jackson was his brand of makeup and underwear.

On Martin Luther King Day, January 17, Michael hosted one hundred children at his ranch from the Community Youth Sports and Arts Foundation. The media was barred with the exception of Los Angeles TV station KCAL and BET, the Black Entertainment Network. All of the children interviewed said Michael was very kind and lots of fun to be with. None of them believed he was guilty of harming any child.

The NAACP Image Awards were held on January 22 and broadcast on February 5. Making a surprise appearance was their 1993 Entertainer of the Year, Michael Jackson, in his first professional appearance since returning home from Europe. He was greeted by deafening cheers and a standing ovation. Dressed in a black military style jacket with red accents and a silver sequined armband, and no sunglasses, he seemed very upbeat, confident and comfortable. He presented the award for Outstanding Choreography but first took the opportunity to say a few words on his own behalf, pausing now and then to tell the cheering fans, "I love you too" and "I love you more!":

Thank you for your warm and generous support. I love you very much.

For decades, the NAACP has stood at the forefront of the struggle for equal justice under the law for all people in our land. They have fought in the lunch rooms of the South, in the hallowed halls of the Supreme Court and the board rooms of corporate America for justice, equality and the very dignity of all mankind. Members of the NAACP have been jailed and even killed in noble pursuit of those ideals upon which our country was founded. None of these goals is more meaningful to me at this time in my life than the notion that everyone is presumed to be innocent and totally innocent until they are charged with a crime and then convicted by a jury of their peers. I never, I never really took the time to understand the importance of that ideal until now, until I became the victim of false allegations and the willingness of others to believe the worst before they have a chance to hear the truth. Because not only am I presumed innocent, I am innocent! And I know the truth will be my salvation. You have been there to support me when others weren't around and I thank you for that. I have been strengthened in my fight to prove my innocence by my faith in God and by my knowledge that

I am not fighting this battle alone. Together, we will see this thing through and I'm very proud to be here.

And now it is my distinct honor to announce the recipient of the first NAACP Image Award for Outstanding Choreography in film or television...

He then announced the winner, Debbie Allen. Allen immediately invited her fellow nominees to the stage which included Michael Peters, nominated for his work on *What's Love Got To Do With It*. Peters ascended the stairs to the stage and immediately went to his friend Michael Jackson and hugged him warmly. Allen began her acceptance speech saying, "God bless you Michael, we're all on your side."

A two page ad was placed in the program for the 26th Annual NAACP Image Awards, one page was a photo of Michael Jackson, the opposite page read, "Michael, I love you. - Elizabeth".

Talk show newcomer Bertice Berry featured the Michael Jackson story a couple of times on her show. One such show airing in January featured a former chef from Neverland, Johnny Ciao. In this particular show Ciao, who has worked for several celebrities in the past, said he never saw anything strange at the ranch, and that he has seen more eccentricities with other stars than he has working for Michael Jackson. In other interviews Ciao's story seemed to change, probably according to how much money he was being paid.

Reporter Florence Anthony appeared on the show and continued her efforts to support and defend Michael at every opportunity. The investigative reporter who first broke the story, Don Ray, described how he first became aware of the investigation of Michael Jackson. He also admitted the resulting media lynching of the superstar made him embarrassed to be a journalist. Anthony echoed his feelings.

The music editor for *Vibe* magazine, Alan Light, said he could not defend the St. Louis radio station for pulling Michael Jackson's music from their playlist stating, "there is no trial starting here." Michael Jackson impersonator Valentino described how he had been treated since the allegations became public, with people making rude comments to him, just because he looks like Jackson. A Jackson fan and audience member demonstrated her support for Michael displaying bumper stickers reading "Pepsi dumped Michael, We're dumping Pepsi".

The show's biggest embarrassment was undoubtedly the presence of private investigator Ernie Rizzo, who still claimed to be working for the boy's father. As usual, Rizzo made statements concerning things such as who has and hasn't shared a bed with Michael Jackson that he couldn't possibly know.

Since August 24, 1993 there had been virtually nonstop attention paid by the media to the legal troubles of Michael Jackson. Even in the occasional story not related to the allegations, they were always mentioned. *Every* conceivable aspect of his life had been analyzed, speculated upon, manipulated and interpreted by the media in search of the almighty ratings point or higher circulation. With all the attention focused on the civil suit and the criminal investigation against Michael Jackson, it was virtually ignored by the media that there were actually two different criminal investigations being conducted. A criminal investigation into attempts to extort money from Michael Jackson had also been continuing for these many months against Evan Chandler and his then attorney Barry Rothman. The tapes of phone conversations with Chandler, and other evidence, did not offer the hard evidence of extortion that Pellicano had hoped and after five months of investigation, the Los Angeles prosecutors office announced on January 24, that they were declining to file charges of extortion against the dentist.

Los Angeles Deputy District Attorney Michael Montagna in his announcement noted that trying to settle a civil suit out of court is not a crime and in fact is encouraged by the law. An important point here is that at the beginning of his negotiations with Jackson, Chandler wanted money to keep from making allegations of child abuse public, not to settle a civil suit. There was no civil suit at the time. Chandler only filed a civil action after he was unable to secure his film deals privately.

On January 25, 1994, the rumblings in the press that a settlement was in the works for the civil suit were proven correct. The day before, Feldman filed court documents stating the boy's parents had resigned as guardians over the boy's affairs. A retired Appellate Court Judge, Justice Jack Goertzen, had been named as the boy's new guardian. This is standard procedure in this type of situation and helped to confirm that a settlement had indeed been reached. Chandler had agreed to drop the civil suit in return in for an undisclosed sum of money. The amount of this settlement would be speculated upon by virtually everyone with a typewriter and the amounts would range from $5 million to $100 million, with each being reported with certainty, having come from "an inside source." Basically the amount of the settlement was not to be disclosed and the vast majority of the press were reporting various figures as fast as they could think them up. LaToya, predictably, even had her two cents to chip in, telling the tabloids that the amount of the settlement was actually $50 million to be paid over ten years. For someone who has been estranged from her family for a number of years, she sure does manage to get a hold of a lot of confidential information!

But like everything else connected with this case, there were the consistent "leaks" of information. The most credible and reliable sources claimed the actual amount of the settlement was $10 million, with $1 million going directly to Chandler, the remaining $9 million being put in a trust fund for Jordy. Reportedly part of the settlement states that there can be no books published by the immediate family. Without hesitation however it was revealed that the boy's uncle was meeting with publishers. The boy needs to begin healing, he can't go through the ordeal of a trial. But he can certainly pocket a few million dollars and then relive the whole thing for the whole world to read so even more money can be made.

It later became known that the settlement may not have to be paid by Michael Jackson at all. A claim had been filed with Transamerica Insurance, suppliers of Michael Jackson's personal liability insurance. A spokesperson for the insurance company said the claim would be reviewed, and if found to be valid, it would pay.

Two hundred and fifty reporters and camera crews crowded outside the Superior Court building for the announcement of the settlement. Attorneys for both sides made statements and each side reiterated that the settlement was in no way an admission of any guilt by Michael Jackson. Larry Feldman addressed the assembled masses stating it was time for his client to start the healing process:

> *We wish to jointly announce a mutual resolution of this lawsuit. As you are aware, the plaintiff has alleged certain acts of impropriety by Mr. Jackson. And from the inception of those allegations, Mr. Jackson has always maintained his innocence. However the emotional trauma and strain on the respective parties have caused both parties to reflect on the wisdom of continuing with this litigation. The plaintiff has agreed that the lawsuit should be resolved and it will be dismissed in the near future. While Mr. Jackson continues to maintain his innocence, he withdraws any previous allegations of extortion. This will allow the parties to get on with their lives in a more positive and productive manner.*
>
> *Much of the suffering these parties have been put through was caused by the publicity surrounding this case. We jointly request that members of the press allow the parties to close this chapter of their lives with dignity.*

Johnnie Cochran also addressed the media stating again that the settlement was no admission of guilt on behalf of Michael Jackson:

> *In the past 10 days the rumors and speculation surrounding this case have reached a fever pitch and, by and large, have been false and outrageous. As Mr. Feldman has correctly indicated, Michael Jackson has maintained his innocence from the beginning of this matter and now as this matter will soon be concluded, he still maintains that innocence.*

The resolution of this case is in no way an admission of guilt by Michael Jackson. In short, he is an innocent man who does not intend to have his career and his life destroyed by rumors and innuendos. Throughout this ordeal, he has been subjected to an unprecedented media feeding frenzy, especially by the tabloid press. The tabloid press has shown an insatiable thirst for anything negative and has paid huge sums of money to people who have little or no information and who barely knew Michael Jackson.

So today, the time has come for Michael Jackson to move on to new business, to get on with his life, to start the healing process and to move his career forward to even greater heights. This he intends to do. At the appropriate time, Michael Jackson will speak out publicly as to the agony, torture and pain he has had to suffer during the past six months.

Both sides insisted that the settling of the civil action would have no impact on the continuing criminal investigation, that "no one's silence was bought". However, having gotten the cash they were after, there was no motivation for the boy to testify in any criminal action. From the very start of the whole thing, they were only interested in getting paid, not justice for the alleged harm done to the boy, no punishment for Michael, or the well being of the boy, only cash. Numerous legal experts began appearing on news programs and talk shows explaining that the settlement in the civil suit would effectively end the criminal investigation. With no reason for the "victim" to testify, there was no evidence, only hearsay testimony, most likely not enough to justify filing criminal charges.

Los Angeles District Attorney Gil Garcetti maintained however that the settlement of the civil suit did not affect the criminal investigation. He refused to give up on the now five month investigation that so far had yielded no evidence to justify filing criminal charges against Michael Jackson. The case seemed further impeded by the fact that California law did not allow the state to compel testimony from juveniles in sex crime cases. One week after the settlement was announced, Garcetti announced that he would sponsor legislation to force sexual assault victims to testify in criminal cases even if they sue their alleged assailants for money. Obviously without the testimony of the boy, their case against Michael was non-existent. Now that he had a few million bucks lining his pocket there was no motivation to testify in any criminal proceeding. They had already gotten what they wanted, money. Therefore Garcetti had to try to change the law of California to force the boy to testify.

DeWayne Wickham, a columnist for Gannett News Service and *USA Today*, consistently offered insight into the investigation and questioned the motives of the media as well as the investigators. Wickham questioned the media's willingness to convict Michael without any evidence against him while ignoring the more plausible claims of extortion against the dentist. One article, "Officials desperate to nail Michael Jackson", focused on the extreme measures being taken by investigators to find something incriminating against Michael. Wickham asked, assuming Garcetti was successful in amending the laws of California forcing the boy to testify and he still refused, what would he do, put the boy in jail? The law enforcement officials in Santa Barbara, being equally desperate, arranged for the thirteen year old son of Michael's former maid to see a therapist. This offer was made after the mother complained and said she felt uncomfortable with the police questioning her son alone. The police had questioned the boy after his mother said he had spent time with Michael. The police had meetings with the boy and made phone calls to him when his mother was not home. The boy has repeatedly denied being abused in any way.

All along the investigators seemed to be going to extremes to find something, anything, to incriminate Michael. For the body search of Michael, the Santa Barbara District Attorney wanted several police officers present and even wanted to use a ruler to measure the size of any spots on his skin! Michael's attorney were successful in getting these excessive and desperate demands denied.

Tom Sneddon, the Santa Barbara District Attorney, later filed a motion in court to obtain Michael Jackson's medical records from his dermatologist. He wanted to compare earlier photos of Michael with the more recent ones taken during the body search. It seemed they were still clinging to the possibility that Michael had undergone cosmetic surgery while he was out of the country for four weeks in late 1993.

The immediate reaction to the announcement of the settlement by some of the media and general public, was that it indicated guilt on the behalf of Michael Jackson. This is a very hasty conclusion. There are many, many factors to consider on both sides of the case before coming to such a potentially damaging conclusion. Immediately many felt Michael must be guilty if he was willing to pay the kid off, buying his silence. No thought was given to the boy and his father's willingness to accept a stack of cash to forget that the boy had been sexually abused. Will that make everything all better? There has been no indication from Chandler that he was ever interested in Michael Jackson being punished for what he had supposedly done to his boy, no indication that Chandler was interested in getting his boy's life back on track, no indication in justice at all, only money. The civil suit, asking for monetary damages, was filed against Michael as soon as the allegations became public and Chandler lost all hope of getting his proposed private settlement offer. At the time the allegations first came up Chandler arranged meetings with attorneys and representatives of Michael Jackson and Michael himself to discuss a settlement. He did not go to the police. He did not file any criminal complaint. He asked for money.

Many pointed out that Michael paid the boy off to avoid having to go to trial and testify under oath. But by settling the suit Michael is not the only one who avoided testifying in court. It is a safe bet that Michael was not the only one involved who dreaded the thought of telling their story under oath. Surely, neither party was as eager to go to court as they may have indicated publicly. Imagine the attention a court trial would have drawn to Michael. Details of the most intimate aspects of his personal life, his sexual history, the photos of his nude body, his medical history, and God knows what else would have been paraded through every persons living room throughout the world for days, weeks and months on end. Court TV's CEO Steven Brill had even expressed an interest in carrying the trial live on television. The tabloid shows would have fed off of that for months. It isn't hard to imagine why Michael would want to avoid that.

The makeup of the potential jury had to be a significant concern for each side. Certainly there was not a person who hadn't been in a coma for the last six months who didn't know about the allegations being made against Michael Jackson. With the avalanche of exaggerations, unfounded speculation, and outright lies being sold to the highest bidder in the media war, it has to be considered if members of any jury wouldn't already have a negative view of the case before it ever started. Feldman probably had just the opposite concerns about the jury. Michael Jackson is not just any celebrity. He is regarded throughout the world as not only the greatest entertainer, but as perhaps the most caring humanitarian, especially in regards to children. Certainly some could have already formed views of Michael as being the real victim in the case.

The civil trial itself and what had to be proven put both sides into a very difficult situation. In a criminal proceeding, a jury must come to an *unanimous* decision that a crime was committed *beyond a reasonable doubt*. Neither of these factors are required in a civil case. In a civil proceeding, a unanimous decision by the jury is not required. Further, the jury in a civil proceeding need only find that a preponderance of evidence suggests that a crime was committed. This effectively put Michael in the difficult position of having to prove his innocence. How do you prove that something did not happen?

While the prosecution did not have to convince every juror, and didn't have to convince them beyond a reasonable doubt, the boy still faced the possibility of having to tell details of his story in court. Under oath. And he had very little to work with. The whole case was based on the testimony of a minor in the middle of a

bitter custody battle, one of the most unreliable witnesses according to some legal experts. He also faced a
grueling cross-examination by Jackson's attorneys. The
only thing that halfway supported his side were former
employees of Neverland who would testify that Michael
did spend time with children, and a chauffeur, Gary
Hearne, who testified in his deposition that he had
driven Michael to the boy's house at night and picked
him up in the morning for a period of about thirty days.
The prosecution had to offer the alleged victim, and a
handful of ex-employees none of whom, for all of their
paid "exclusive" interviews, ever saw any improper
behavior on behalf of Michael Jackson. Ever. And
their credibility would certainly be destroyed when the
jury learned they had been paid for their stories. The
defense on the other hand, if need be, could line up
character witnesses that would put Hands Across
America to shame. Evan Chandler and his son could
very well go through the stressful ordeal of a trial to end
up without getting a penny. And with the incessant
media attention, it would have virtually impossible to
continue to keep the boy's identity from being revealed
worldwide.

Still another fact that many were unaware of, is
that 95% of all civil cases are settled without going to
court. In fact, the law encourages the parties involved
to do so. This civil case being settled out of court,
therefore, is by no means unusual.

On January 25, President Bill Clinton delivered
his State of the Union address. Accordingly, that same
night, ABC's *Nightline,* was devoted to the topic of, well,
Michael Jackson. Ted Koppel's guests included Larry
Feldman, attorney Raoul Felder, and former Los
Angeles District Attorney Ira Reiner. Felder stated he

believed that the money paid to the boy would effectively prevent his testifying in any criminal case. The possibility was also raised that Feldman purposely publicized the case to put added pressure on Michael Jackson to settle the case.

Feldman's assertion that his client wanted to settle the case so he could put the matter behind him and begin healing was also questioned. If the settlement, as Feldman stated himself, did not buy the boy's silence, then accepting the money didn't really relieve him of any burden to testify in court.

Raoul Felder said of the settlement, "It basically says that if you throw money at the scales of justice, it bends your way." The settlement was a *two way agreement*. Michael didn't have to shove his money down Chandler's throat. He willingly took the money, it was what he had been after for months. As for the scales of justice bending his way, there has been no instance in which Michael Jackson was given any special treatment due to his fame or his wealth. But it certainly seemed to bring him undue public scrutiny and the automatic assumption of guilt.

Following the settlement, many law experts questioned why it took so long. Insiders said it was due to the advice Michael was receiving from Bert Fields and Anthony Pellicano. Colleagues said Fields was against negotiating a settlement because it would be seen as an indication of guilt. He also wanted the opportunity to cross-examine the boy. Johnnie Cochran, seen as being shrewder about limiting the amount of damage done, did not oppose a settlement. As soon as Cochran took over for Fields, he began negotiating the settlement. Legal experts speculated that had Cochran been representing

Michael Jackson at the beginning, it wouldn't have gotten so out of control.

Coinciding with the announcement of the settlement, Johnny Ciao, Michael's former chef, became the latest to cash a *Hard Copy* check in doing his interview with Diane Dimond. In the interview Ciao said he never saw any improper behavior, but that parents would accompany their children to the ranch, and then the children would spend time with Michael and Ciao was left to entertain the parents. In other interviews, as described earlier, Ciao told a very different story. Interestingly, only in his interview with Diane Dimond did he come off as doubting Michael.

A Current Affair's Mike Watkiss uttered these words in reporting on the settlement of the civil case, (they are printed here verbatim so as not to distort his meaning by paraphrasing):

The very thought of someone like Michael Jackson being able to buy his way out of a disturbing situation like these ugly child sex abuse allegations I think is troubling for most people who see it as a calculated effort to thwart justice and yet another example of how the rich and powerful can play by another set of rules than you and me. Yet if we listen to the words of Michael's sister LaToya, it may not be the first time the eccentric superstar has found himself in the position of forking over large sums of cash...

Old footage of LaToya claiming she saw checks for "large sums" made payable to the parents of children was then rebroadcast.

There are numerous problems with Watkiss' statement. Michael Jackson absolutely did not buy himself out of any trouble. If Michael was interested in buying himself out of trouble, why did he not give the money to Chandler seven months ago and avoid the allegations being made public, and the subsequent media fiasco in which Watkiss played such a large role?

Watkiss' statement raises multiple questions. Just how did Michael Jackson thwart justice? And how does Watkiss know what other people think is troubling? What other set of rules did Michael Jackson play by? A civil suit was only filed because he is rich and powerful. If he were John Doe, steel mill worker in Gary, Indiana, a multi million dollar civil suit would never have been filed. Finally, Watkiss listens to the words of LaToya, which change from one day to the next, and than calls Michael eccentric?! Easily the most troubling aspect of this story is now nonsense such as this ever makes the airwaves.

The announcement of the settlement quieted the media drastically. It also seemed to sour one business deal. LaToya then backed out of a deal with St. Martin's Press for a book about her brother who she loves so dearly.

With the civil suit finally settled, the media continued to speculate on whether the settlement was an indication of Michael's guilt. Throughout the whole ugly ordeal, the media continually doubted every word uttered by Michael and his representatives, and they were consistently proven wrong. When concert dates at the beginning of the Asian leg of the Dangerous tour were canceled due to Michael's illness, it was questioned in the media if he was really ill. Crew members backstage at the show saw him double over in pain and collapse, due to a migraine headache. He was then admitted to a hospital and underwent a MRI. When shows in Mexico City were canceled due to Michael suffering a toothache, that too was questioned by the press. But, Michael was admitted to a hospital, ABC Hospital, and underwent oral surgery to remove an abscessed tooth. When the remaining tour dates were canceled, and Michael released his statement that he was seeking treatment for an addiction to painkillers, the press went crazy with stories doubting his addiction and coming up with alternative motives for him to end the tour and stay out of the country. They were proven wrong again. Michael's treatment for an addiction to painkillers was verified by the doctor treating him, Dr. Beauchamp Colclough. As soon as the tour was canceled and Michael remained out of the country, there was massive speculation that he would never return to the United States. Michael did of course return, just as he and his attorneys said he would, on December 10. Michael surprised the media yet again when he did in fact personally and publicly address the allegations being made against him and publicly declared his complete and total innocence on December 22.

It is also important to consider how closely the actions of Michael's accuser followed the statements made by Anthony Pellicano on August 24, 1993, when the whole thing hit the fan. Pellicano stated the allegations were brought as the result of a failed extortion attempt by the father. It has since been proven that Chandler did indeed engage in negotiations for film deals in return for not making the allegations public. Pellicano, Michael's attorneys and Michael Jackson himself consistently maintained the allegations were brought as an attempt to get money, nothing else. As soon as the civil suit was settled, Jordy refused to cooperate with prosecutors. Nothing in the settlement prevented the boy from testifying in any criminal proceeding. Chandler could have had the money *and* cooperated with efforts to prosecute Michael. But he didn't. He just took the money. It was learned through Pellicano that Chandler, from the very beginning, wanted to secure several film deals so he could then disolve his dental practice and work on his screenplays full time. Shortly after the settlement in the civil suit was reached, Chandler left his dental practice.

Those in the media who speculated that the settlement of the civil suit would do irreparable damage to Michael's career will be proven wrong again. Michael can, and has in the past, repaired damage to his image and has done so with relative ease. After months of unrelenting media bashing, Michael sent the public's support of him skyrocketing, all in four minutes on CNN on December 22. After literally years of people believing his actually bought the elephant man's bones, slept in a hyperbaric chamber, and bleached his skin, Michael changed lots of people's perspective of him after talking with Oprah Winfrey for ninety minutes on February 10, 1993. Many people who had thought of him as a weirdo now saw him as a person. He will undoubtedly do the same following the many months of media hell he has been put through. Michael Jackson is in no way washed up. He will undoubtedly come back, bigger, better and stronger than ever. Jackson biographer J. Randy Taraborrelli agreed, saying, "The Michael Jackson redemption of 1995 will be something to behold."

While most of the media focused on the settlement of the civil suit with the attitude that Michael had bought himself out of having to go to trial, such as *People* magazine's cover story, "Michael's Dangerous Deal", *Jet* magazine took a more humane and realistic view. Michael was featured on the cover of their

February 14, 1994 issue with the headline, "Michael Jackson Settles Suit, Maintains Innocence And Gets On With His Life."

Just after settling the civil suit and in getting on with his life, Michael Jackson hired a new publicist, Michael Levine. Levine would work in partnership with Lee Solters. Levine had worked with Michael earlier in his career.

As an indication of how very weak the case against Michael was, a source told Reuters News Service on January 27, that the photos taken of Michael Jackson's genitals did not match the description his accuser had given to police. As an indication of how fair and objective the coverage of the "Michael Jackson Scandal" was handled by the media, the report that the photos of Michael's body did not match the boy's description was buried in the back pages of newspapers and ignored by the tabloid TV shows.

6

Long Live the King

MTV was among those who refused to give up on Michael Jackson. While they could have easily dropped his videos from airing on the video network, they continued to not only air the videos, but to showcase Michael's videos in various specials and "Michael Jackson Weekends" where his videos and specials were spotlighted for an entire weekend. On January 29, 1994, the Top 100 You Make the Call Countdown was held in which viewers called in and voted for their favorite video. The votes determined the top five videos on the countdown. "Thriller" was voted by viewers as the fourth top video.

Michael's star on the Hollywood Walk of Fame was defaced on February 1. The culprit who sprayed the star with fluorescent orange paint was chased and caught by a witness and held for police! Jose Gomez was arrested and subsequently sentenced to one hundred days in jail for vandalism. The star was immediately cleaned up and was good as new in no time. Gomez said he did it because he hates child molesters. He didn't say why he didn't then vent his anger on an actual child molester.

On February 2, Michael made another public appearance. He attended a concert of the Fifth Dimension and the Temptations at the Sheraton Desert Inn in Las Vegas. He attended the concert with Lisa Marie Presley, Elvis' daughter. The hotel had received a call earlier in the day letting them know Michael was coming. The King of Pop and the daughter of the King of Rock and Roll were seated in a VIP section known as "King's row".

On the legal front, Michael's lawyers fought for the return of Michael's medical records. Investigators had evidently not found whatever they had been looking for in the records, no more evidence of anything was uncovered. Cochran claimed Michael agreed to hand over the records only temporarily. Prosecutors claimed the waiver of rights was indefinite.

The February 5, 1994 issue of *Billboard* outlined the overwhelming support Michael was receiving from the music industry. Sony was standing by their earlier statements of support for Michael. His *Greatest Hits* album had now been postponed for the umpteenth time in favor of a whole new album. Record chain owners reported sales of Michael Jackson's albums had actually *increased.* KEZK-FM in St. Louis had not yet to decide to lift their ban on his music, but most radio station DJ's, record store owners, and industry insiders felt Michael Jackson's career would continue to flourish. Most radio listeners said they would buy Michael Jackson's records and would go to his concerts.

Following his victory in the recent copyright suit for "Thriller", "The Girl is Mine" and "We Are The World", a similar suit began in U.S. District Court in Denver, Colorado, on February 7. Crystal Cartier was suing Michael for pirating the song "Dangerous" from her. Cartier said she wrote the song in 1985 and recorded it in October, 1990. She claimed further that she had sent out twenty five copies of her version of the song to record companies, but she could not locate an original copy of the demo for the trial. She wanted to use a re-created version of the song in court. Judge Edward Nottingham said he wouldn't allow the reconstructed tape to be used in court unless it could be shown that "adequate attempts" had been made to locate an original copy. Cartier claimed Michael Jackson, MJJ Productions, Sony Music Entertainment and Epic Records violated copyright and trademark laws.

During the second day of the trial, Denver musician Kris Farris, an expert witness for the plaintiff, testified, "I think the most important similarity is in the choruses of the songs. And the most obvious similarity is the use of the word, 'dangerous'". Michael's attorney challenged each likeness and asked if Farris was aware that there have been over two hundred songs copyrighted in the United States since the mid 1930's with the title, "Dangerous". Farris, according to the testimony, was unaware of this. It turns out "Dangerous" is not that original of a title after all.

On Monday, February 14, fans waited in line outside the Denver courtroom to see Michael Jackson who had gone to Denver to testify in the copyright case to defend his work. At one point, Cartier, who was dressed in a tight and much too revealing leather minidress, was sent home by the judge to change into something more appropriate for court.

In his testimony, Michael described his song-writing techniques, and how long he has been composing songs. He testified that he began composing music at the age of seven and had his first song published at the age of fifteen. To date he said he has written "in general, a couple of hundred" songs. Of those, fifty to sixty have been released to the public. He testified that approximately sixty to seventy songs were written for the *Bad* album, and "I think seventy" songs were written for the *Dangerous* album. The songs that do not end up on an album are then stored in a vault. Sometimes they are brought out again and used in creating a new song, as was "Dangerous", which evolved out of an earlier song, "Street Walker", "I wrote a song for the *Bad* album called "Street Walker" and it had a driving base melody, a strong driving base lick. That base lick was taken by the engineer and put new chords to the base lick."

Michael testified that the chords added to the base lick of "Street Walker" inspired him to write the melody of "Dangerous". He demonstrated how the base sounded on "Street Walker" and how he then wrote the vocal melody, singing parts of the music of "Dangerous". Michael demonstrated how he creates a vocal melody by using another song he wrote as an example, "When creating the song 'Billie Jean', I was riding in my car and it started with the base lick again, which goes (he sings the base sounds of "Billie Jean" a capella) and on top of that I hear the chords (he sings the chords of "Billie Jean") and then the melody, 'She was more like a beauty queen from a movie scene, I said don't mind, but do you mean I am the one...' And the lyrics, the strings, the chords come together at that moment like a gift that is put right into your head and that's how I hear it."

Michael testified that he does not read or write sheet music, "No, I don't. I don't think it's necessary." He also testified that he alone wrote the lyrics and melody to "Dangerous", and that he alone titled it "Dangerous". He stated he had never before heard Cartier's version of the song. Asked if he was positive, he replied, "I am more than positive. It's the honest truth." He sang portions of "Dangerous" showing how he created the melody after hearing the chords that were added to the base lick by Bill Boutrell. He also recalled the first time he sang the lyrics to "Dangerous" in the recording studio with other people present:

> *It was kind of a funny day, not really funny, but... I usually like to sing in the dark because I like to just feel everything and I don't like people looking at me unless I'm on stage. And so, all the lights were off. And right before I started singing, this huge, I think it was seven feet tall, this huge wall fell right on my head. It made a loud banging sound. It hurt. But I didn't realize how much it hurt me until the next day. I was kind of dizzy. But it's pretty much on tape. If you play the demo of us working on 'Dangerous', it was even recorded.*

The demo tape of "Dangerous" was then played in the courtroom, with a loud banging noise at the very beginning of the tape. Michael testified that the lyrics and vocal melody of the song never changed from the time this demo was recorded to the release of the album. Bill Boutrell added chords to the bass lick which inspired the melody for Michael and Teddy Riley updated the sounds of the instruments, giving it "more feeling and emotion".

It was pointed out that themes of love being dangerous, and women being dangerous have been repeated in past songs of Michael's. "Dirty Diana", written in 1985-1986, and "Billie Jean", written in 1982, each deal with a dangerous woman. "Smooth Criminal", which Michael wrote in 1985-1986, uses police sirens and machine gun sounds. Each of these were composed before Cartier recorded her song "Dangerous". Michael also demonstrated how the music of a portion of "Another Part of Me", from the *Bad* album released in 1987, is the same as a portion of "Dangerous".

Michael testified that he has a strict policy of not accepting unsolicited tapes. "I do not take unsolicited tapes. What happens when you do something like that is this situation." He said he only accepts songs from well known songwriters with a track record of success, citing Rod Temperton and Stevie Wonder as examples.

Cartier's attorney then began cross-examining Michael, asking many questions which he had just answered. Did he write the lyrics to "Dangerous"? Did anyone assist in that process? Did Bill Boutrell write any of the lyrics? Did Teddy Riley write any of the lyrics of "Dangerous"? He was even asked again if he read sheet music, "No, I don't. Neither did Lennon and McCartney. It's not necessary." "Do you write sheet music?" "No, I don't do that. It's not necessary." Cartier's attorney had Michael thumb through an exhibit of a track sheet used in recording in which the pages in Michael's copy were different than the one held by the attorney. After figuring out the page she meant, Michael read the dates listed on the sheet used in the recording of "Dangerous", 2-1-91 for tracks one through six.

Referring to the deposition Michael gave for the case, Cartier's attorney tried to show Michael's testimony in court differed from the statements he made in the deposition. When Michael was asked where "Dangerous" was recorded, he replied, "Recording for 'Dangerous' was done, I'm not sure, it could have been Record One Studio...I'm not sure, I record at a lot of studios." The attorney then read from Michael's deposition, "Question: 'Was any of the recording done at Record One?' Answer: 'I do not know.'" The attorney then told the court that these two terms were, to her, inconsistent!

After only 3 1/2 hours of deliberation, the jury found in favor of Michael Jackson, that he was the creator of "Dangerous" and he did not steal the song from Cartier. A few weeks later, refusing to give up on that $40 million, Cartier asked the court for a time extension in which to file her appeal so she could raise the $5,000 needed to pursue the appeal.

Just after the completion of this copyright case, the public was ordering copies of Michael's latest release, his testimony from the case! The U.S. District Court in Denver was flooded with orders for a fifty minute audio cassette of Michael's testimony in which he sings portions of "Billie Jean" and "Dangerous". The cassettes, priced at $15, were reported to be selling very well and some reports joked it was climbing the charts. The judge in the case, Judge Edward W. Nottingham, is one of three judges, out of eight, in the courthouse who use electronic court reporters, making the cassettes possible. Funds raised from the sale of the tape were put in a general fund of the U.S. Treasury. Representatives of Michael's acknowledged the court's right to make the tapes available to the public.

Some in the media questioned why Michael would fight so vigorously to protect his music, but avoided going to court to defend himself against the allegations of molestation being made against him. Again the same considerations have to be made. During the testimony for the copyright case, Michael was questioned on how long he has been composing music, how he writes songs in general, and how he came to compose "Dangerous" and other songs. There was not one question concerning his personal life, his sexual activity, and not one nude photo of Michael was brought into evidence.

Following Michael's second victory in connection with copyright infringement accusations, Geraldo Rivera aired yet another program focusing on "The Trials of Michael Jackson". A portion of the program centered on the molestation accusations. *New York Post* columnist Cindy Adams appeared on the program and stated that she believes Michael is innocent and had maintained so in her column. Florence Anthony made the very important and valid point that the father only wanted money, not help for his son, not revenge, but money. Contradicting their views, as always, was Ernie Rizzo.

The balance of the program then focused on the accusations of plagiarism, "Did he really write all those songs?" Crystal Cartier, Reynaud Jones and Robert Smith, and Fred Sanford each appeared on the program, convinced Michael Jackson had stolen their songs. Each case has gone to court and Michael Jackson has won each one of the cases, but they seemed to remain convinced, even though Jones and Smith, and Sanford each claim Michael stole "The Girl is Mine" from them.

Determined to not let the settlement of the civil suit hinder the criminal investigation, a grand jury was called in Santa Barbara County to hear testimony from over twelve people. Of the nineteen jurors, twelve of them had to be convinced there existed probable cause that Michael had behaved improperly to justify filing criminal charges against Michael. The first to testify before the grand jury was Miko Brando, son of Marlon Brando, who had worked for MJJ Productions as a bodyguard and had become close friends with Michael. Brando was questioned by the grand jury for 3 1/2 hours. MJJ Productions executive Norma Staikos was also among the first to testify before the grand jury. Others who were called to testify before the grand jury were James DeBarge, Janet's former husband who lived at Hayvenhurst during their four month marriage, Dr. Arnold Klein's personal trainer, who had accompanied Klein to Mexico City in November, chauffeur Gary Hearne, and Joy Robson, the mother of Michael's young friend, Wade Robson.

With the grand jury convening in Santa Barbara, the scandal hungry tabloid TV shows once again kicked into high gear. *A Current Affair* offered up an interview with attorney Gloria Allred for her perspective on the story. What an objective, impartial observer - an attorney who had represented the boy at the beginning of the whole thing!

The very next day, the same scandal show featured a dramatization of the supposed seduction by Michael Jackson of the boy. The dramatization included portions of depositions taken from two housekeepers, Gail Goforth and Adrian McManus who were both described as hostile witnesses, Blanca Francia, as well as footage of a Michael Jackson impersonator with a young boy. This infuriated Michael's attorneys who hoped to encourage Michael to sue the show.

The show's host, Maureen O'Boyle, appeared via satellite on the *Bertice Berry Show* to defend her show, where she was repeatedly verbally attacked by audience members for her show's disregard for ethics. Questioned about the fairness in airing the program after the case had been settled, O'Boyle claimed the story was balanced. O'Boyle maintained that the dramatization, featuring a Michael Jackson look-a-like with a young boy, was based on the deposition of the boy. In a taped interview, Johnnie Cochran stated there was never a deposition taken from the boy. Cochran stated further that in her deposition for the civil case, the maid stated she never did see Michael Jackson in the shower with anybody, and she never saw Michael Jackson molest anybody.

Other guests on the *Bertice Berry Show* included journalist Florence Anthony, Steve Manning, Lo-Mae Lai, a reporter for the *Globe* and a former attorney, also showing up again, like a bad penny, was Ernie Rizzo. Anthony continued to staunchly support Michael stating that it was obvious at this point that there was no evidence against Michael Jackson. Lo-Mae Lai stated that although the story by *A Current Affair* was tacky, they did have a right to air it. Steve Manning condemned the media's coverage of the *Jackson Family Honors* pointing out there was an incredible eight minute ovation for Michael, and that the fans did not boo him as it was reported.

O'Boyle asserted that her show was telling the sequence of events, not forming opinions. Very specific examples of the show's one-sided and tainted stories have been examined here. An audience member told

O'Boyle that her show was done in "bad taste", and felt that it was a disgrace that Rizzo was making money off this case.

Diane Dimond from the often times worse *Hard Copy*, pointed out to the TV audience on her show that a grand jury convening is the first step in indicting a person of a crime. This is true. It is also true however that it could also very well be, finally, the end of the criminal investigation in Santa Barbara once and for all. But she never mentioned that.

Despite his various legal hassles, Michael kept a promise he had made to the citizens of Krindjabo during his visit to the village in the Ivory Coast, West Africa, in February 1992. While there, Michael was crowned "King of the Sanwis", an honor which had been given only to visiting dignitaries. Michael had promised to build a cultural center for the village. And he didn't forget them. Ethce Elleingand, mayor of Oboisso, a representative of the King of Krindjabo, visited Neverland Valley. Upon his return home, Elleingand told the press ground-breaking on the center would take place very soon in front of the press in Abidjan, Ivory Coast.

The American Music Awards were held on February 7, where Michael Jackson had two nominations. He was nominated for Favorite Pop/Rock Male Artist and Favorite R&B/Soul Male Artist. The Pop Male Artist went to Eric Clapton and the R&B award went to Luther Vandross. The Michael Jackson International Artist Award which had been created and named for Michael in 1993, was presented to Rod Stewart. Michael did not attend.

Never at a loss for ridiculous stories to print, the *London Daily Mirror* carried a story in February that Michael was filing a $455 million lawsuit against LaToya for defamation of character. Jack Gordon said that Michael's camp had threatened the lawsuit and that he and LaToya would countersue Michael. LaToya told *Geraldo*, in a taped telephone call as a preface for a rerun of a show with LaToya, that the story was made up by the tabloid and she had not been served with any papers. She also stated that her husband had called the Jacksons and threatened to sue for $1 billion and take Joe to court in Indiana for the molestation of his daughter. As usual, the whole story was false, Michael never threatened to sue his sister for any of her remarks about him. What would be the point of filing a lawsuit if, according to some of the same tabloids, he was planning to have her killed?!

After talking with LaToya and her statement that the story was made up, Geraldo ran a teaser for his rerun claiming it was the show "so explosive" that got LaToya slapped with a $455 million lawsuit threat. Actually there was no lawsuit, no threat of a lawsuit, only Geraldo bending the facts to hype the rerun.

Taking a different spin on the story was a show on PBS, *Frontline*, which instead of focusing on the story itself, focused on the media's coverage of a big story, using the Michael Jackson story as an example. Reported by Pulitzer Prize winner Richard Ben Cramer, it is pointed out that the important thing in reporting this story, and others like it, is not that the facts are true, just that they are sensational enough to make money, "When news and entertainment is all one business, there is no wall between fiction and fact, as long as it's good commerce." The show centered on the insane turn of events and the unconscionable greed that propelled the story. *Everybody* was for sale regardless if what they had to say had any merit whatsoever. People were only out

for money and the tabloid magazines and TV shows
were only too happy to shell out a few dollars to get a
good story. They had no concern over if a story was
true, only that they had someone to *say* it was true.
Paul Barresi helped to deliver a couple of former
Jackson employees to a London tabloid only because he
was promised a percentage of their fee. He readily
admitted this and had absolutely no problem with it,
"My interest in helping them was that they promised me
a percentage of what they got. I was not on any kind of
crusade to bring anyone to justice, and whether Michael
was guilty or innocent at that point was inconsequential."
     Network news veteran Walter Cronkite agreed
that paying people for their stories greatly distorts the
truth, the facts become buried by sensationalism and
greed. "I think by gosh, that we ought to have an FCC
rule that anytime anybody's paid for an interview, the
price should be superimposed right under their face on
the screen...If we were told what people had been paid
for these stories, we might be able to better judge their
truth or falsity."
     The days leading up to the taping of the *Jackson
Family Honors* were filled with conflicting reports on just
who was and was not going to attend, who was going to
perform, where the proceeds would be donated and just
what the whole thing was for. The show was designed
to be an annual event at which awards would be given to
individuals in recognition of their humanitarian efforts.
Those being honored at the first annual *Jackson Family
Honors* were no doubt chosen in part to help insure
Michael's participation.   Elizabeth Taylor is quite
possibly Michael's closet friend, confidante and inspiration.   Berry Gordy, certainly not Joe Jackson's first

choice to honor, has been acknowledged by Michael as being his teacher, friend, and father figure.

The proceeds from the show were said to benefit a variety of charities. Television broadcast fees and ticket revenues were estimated at $6 million. Of this, $500,000 was pledged to charities not controlled by the Jacksons, an entertainment industry earthquake relief fund, Friends of Conservation, and the Library of Congress - American Popular Music Program. The remaining $5.5 million was to go to Jackson Jubilee, Inc. This organization was questioned by some in the media because it was not registered with the IRS. Jackson Communications Inc. CEO, Robert Petrallia responded saying that an application for nonprofit status had been filed with the IRS and it would be resolved in one to two months. LaToya, dispensing some more of her inside knowledge, had charged that the money was actually going to benefit her brothers, who haven't worked for years.

Three days before the scheduled taping of the *Jackson Family Honors*, LaToya told the press that she had not been invited but intended to show up anyway. In complete contrast from earlier statements, she said she wanted to put the differences between herself and her family in the past, "Since it is a family reunion and I am part of the family, I feel I have a right to participate as well." In response, Jermaine, the show's co-producer, told the press that LaToya was welcome, she need only contact her family directly, "An invitation was extended to LaToya for the originally scheduled show in December at which time she never responded. Therefore, if she is truly serious about joining her family in the upcoming charitable event, she needs to contact her family directly. This is a show that is being put together by the Jackson family themselves and not through agents, managers or lawyers."

Jack Gordon meanwhile told *USA Today* that he had heard that Michael would not be attending the show. Neither would Elizabeth Taylor. John McLaughlin, a Jackson family spokesman, put Gordon's comments into perspective, saying "It's interesting he knows so much about a family he never speaks to."

As the show grew nearer, LaToya changed her tune. Again. She stated she would not attend the show because she refused to sign a gag order preventing her from making comments about her family, especially Michael. In a press conference held the morning of the taping, Katherine Jackson, addressed the claim LaToya had made, "If we wanted LaToya to sign a gag order, we would have done it a long time ago." Actually the only thing LaToya needed to sign if she wished to participate was a paper stating what she wanted to do on the show, something each performer provided.

In yet another statement made leading up to the show, LaToya said she and Gordon would show up, dressed as Arabs. At the last minute, they changed their minds. Imagine that. The day of the show, LaToya had yet another story to tell. She told interviewers that the family had hired one hundred additional security guards and had rented five hundred additional walkie talkies to keep her away. Certainly it would impossible for LaToya to slip by a hundred security guards each armed with five walkie talkies.

Speculation over whether or not LaToya would show up only helped to fill pages in newspapers and fill airtime on TV talk shows. The big, and very important, questions were "Is Michael going to be there?" "Is he going to perform?" The answers had a dramatic impact on ticket sales and sales of advertising time. Ticket prices ranged from $150 to $1,000. As the date of the show grew nearer, the extent of Michael's participation varied from one day to the next. At first, it was reported that Michael would appear at the show, but it wasn't certain if he would perform or not. Then Jermaine, the show's co-producer, said Michael would perform with the brothers and do a solo performance. It turned out this was wishful thinking. Next, it was reported that Michael would present awards to Elizabeth Taylor, but would not perform. The day before the show, it was being said that he would present the honor to Taylor and would perform with the brothers, but would not do a solo performance.

The skepticism over whether or not Michael would perform hurt ticket sales. While the $150 to $250 tickets sold out quickly, sales of the higher priced tickets lagged. In the month before the show, the MGM Grand Hotel received over 180,000 phone calls asking if Michael would sing. When they learned he may not, ticket sales tapered off. Two days before the show, the ticket prices were cut by as much as half as Michael's contribution, or even attendance, grew unclear. It left no doubt who people were paying to see.

Some advertising executives claimed that Michael's continuing legal problems would lead them not to recommend the show to their clients. Jerry della Femina, an advertising executive, said he would not recommend the show to his clients because of Michael's recent problems. Jack Curry, Managing Editor of *TV Guide*, predicted you would not see the very big companies advertising on the show, such as fast food chains and toys. He was wrong. Burger King was one of the show's sponsors. Several other large national brands were not scared off from sponsoring the show. Volks-wagen, Pontiac, AT&T, Paramount Pictures, and General Foods were just a few of the sponsors of the show. Probably with no intended pun or statement on the inner turmoil and stress in the Jackson family, Mylanta, Tylenol, and Alka Seltzer were also sponsors of the show. NBC was not worried, "NBC is confident the show will be completely sold out. We're already three-quarters sold now after only ten days."

The day before the taping of the show, *USA Today* carried an interview with Janet, who didn't think it was a good time to stage the show, "I feel that it is very awkward at this time. I called in the beginning and said 'This isn't the right time.' I thought it would be nice to postpone it...but a date was set." She said further that the ordeal with her brother had been very tough on her:

> *You know in your heart what the truth is - he is completely innocent. I stopped listening to the news. They were just sensationalizing everything, lying about this and that. Then you have people you thought were by your side or your friends and they turn against you for money. Now it's kinda died down because there's Tonya Harding. It's always someone.*

She added, "It tore me apart... I would give my left arm, my foot (to prove) he's innocent." Janet also commented on the public's perception that she is normal and Michael is bizarre:

> *If you met my family, you'd see that everyone is very down to earth... What didn't help at all is Mike doesn't speak to the press. When negative things are said about*

him, he never comes forth to defend himself. After that happens so many times, people go, 'Hmmm, maybe it is true.' ... A lot of people feel he doesn't know what's going on in the outside world, when in fact he does. If I had his money, I would build an amusement park at my house too. He is very much an adult, he handles his business very well. What the hell is wrong with still having some kid in you? That's what makes him so wonderful.

Janet also addressed the remarks made in the press by LaToya that she believes the allegations made against Michael:

That's when people feel it's true, when it comes from your own flesh and blood. To me, it's just her way of jumping on something to get attention. Maybe it's because she never had the success she wanted.
    ...What's going on in LaToya's life, I don't even know. I haven't spoken to her in I don't know how long. The person I see on the news and these infomercials is not the person I grew up with.

Janet's remarks are significant because those few reports that did put any credibility to LaToya's comments were because she is a member of Michael's family. Her comments were considered somehow more damaging because she is related to Michael. With these certainly more lucid and more credible statements by Janet refuting LaToya's claims, it seemed to cast an even bigger question mark on LaToya's credibility. LaToya wasn't helping her own case any by today announcing that she would not be attending the reunion show. She was in Las Vegas though, so nobody would really know for sure until showtime.

Finally, after two postponements, and all the controversy, the taping of the *Jackson Family Honors* did take place on February 19, 1994 at the MGM Grand Garden in Las Vegas before a sold out crowd of 15,000. The taping took two hours and forty minutes and was telecast live in twenty eight countries. It was taped for broadcast in the U.S. on February 22. The beginning of the show featured videos shown on a massive set of video screens, including appropriately enough, Michael's "Leave Me Alone". Each appearance of Michael on the screen brought cheers from the audience. But it would be a while before they saw the real thing.

The show opened strongly with a performance of "Alright" from Janet. From there the show dimmed in excitement, as the audience was clearly only waiting it out for the first appearance of the King of Pop.

Other performers on the show included Celine Dion, Smokey Robinson, Dionne Warwick, Gladys Knight, Bruce Hornsby, Another Bad Creation, and comedian Paul Rodriquez. Quincy Jones and Louis Gossett Jr. also appeared. But it wasn't until Smokey Robinson took the stage to introduce Michael that the crowd finally got what they came to see:

It's now my great pleasure to introduce an extraordinarily talented human being. As much as I admire him as a writer and as a performer, I admire him even more as a caring and spiritual person. I've known him since the early days of Motown, and if I knew he was going to become the world's greatest entertainer, I would have treated him a little nicer. I want you all to please welcome 'The King of Pop', Mr. Michael Jackson.

The crowd cheered wildly as Michael walked out on stage to present an award to Berry Gordy. The entire audience rose to their feet. Then they cheered some more. And then some more. It grew louder as Michael acknowledged his fans, waving, blowing kisses, and saying, "I love you!" The standing ovation and the cheering continued for over eight minutes. This crowd wanted to see Michael Jackson. Bad. Really really bad. Michael seemed relaxed and confident, dressed in black jeans, boots, and a black military jacket with a gold leaf pattern down the front, and no sunglasses. He looked healthy and happy, genuinely touched by the love of his fans cheering him. The cheers continued as Michael began to speak, and thanked his fans:

I love you. Thank you. Thank you to the fans. Thank you for your prayers. Thank you for your loyalty. Thank you for your love and your friendship. Mr. Gordy has been an important part of our lives both personally and professionally from the very beginning. He believed in our talent. Like all the other members of the Motown family, we owe our lives and our careers to Berry Gordy, a great human being. We too were very fortunate to benefit of his wisdom, Berry Gordy's commitment and Berry Gordy's creativity. Because of Mr. Gordy and his tireless efforts to get the very best for his artists, to present the very best to the record buying public, the face of popular music has changed forever because of Mr. Gordy. For a lifetime of achievement which includes inspiring so many people with your discipline, philosophy and hard work and the pursuit of a dream, Berry Gordy, I'm proud to present you with the symbol of our love and respect, the Jackson Family Honors. Ladies and gentlemen, a great and incredible human being, Mr. Berry Gordy!

Gordy approached the stage to accept his award but first expressed his love and support for Michael:

> *How time flies. Just the other day you were a nine year old kid auditioning for me and now here you are, the greatest entertainer in the world, presenting me with an award. How wonderful. Thank you, Michael. Michael, I believed in you when you were nine, I believe in you now, and I will never stop believing in you... I am so thrilled to be standing next to not only the greatest entertainer in the world, but one of the most sensitive human beings that ever was and I count him as my most wonderful accomplishments...*

Michael later took the stage again to present the night's second honor to Elizabeth Taylor and again the crowd cheered at his presence as he began to speak:

> *Today we honor Elizabeth Taylor for who she is as much as what she does. For me, Elizabeth Taylor is the ultimate humanitarian because she is the embodiment of love, compassion, faith, and integrity and she has been that ideal for hundreds and millions of fans over the five decades of her illustrious career. Elizabeth began her career when she was nine years old and since then, has starred in some of the greatest of all American films. She has been, and she continues to be, one of the most celebrated women of the twentieth century. I know, from having the honor of being a friend of Elizabeth Taylor's, that she's in no need of another trophy or plaque to recognize her humanitarian work on behalf of the fight against AIDS. And I also know Elizabeth is here tonight not for any ego gratification but because this gives her another chance to get the all important message out to the*

public. The message of AIDS awareness and the need for compassion and the efforts to find a cure. To the formation of AMFAR in 1986 and her own Elizabeth Taylor AIDS Foundation, no one has done more to fight this dreaded disease. But in knowing Elizabeth, I know her reward comes from the work itself, from the small battles won in the all out war, from the gains she's been responsible for by eliminating the problem for the world to see and from the unspoken things of the victims who's lives she has enhanced during their times on earth.

In the midst of my recent trials and tribulations, Elizabeth stood by my side with unwavering strength and support. Elizabeth stands for truth. She's immune to criticism and unfearful to any challenge and places the highest truth in the wisdom of her own heart and the direct knowledge of her own intuition. She is not swayed by public opinion because she knows in the end truth always triumphs. Elizabeth, I love you and we honor you not only for what you stand for, but also for the magnificence of who you are. The world is a better place because of your existence. Because Elizabeth is so unselfish in her devotions to humanity it is doubly fitting that she be the recipient of the Jackson Family Honors award. Ladies and gentlemen, Elizabeth Taylor.

In her acceptance speech, Elizabeth Taylor, directed her comments not toward her humanitarian efforts and the fight for a cure for AIDS, but toward her unending support for her friend in his time of suffering. She also spoke out against the tabloids, asking the public to stop buying the pieces of shi.... garbage. Her damning of the tabloids brought cheers from the crowd with Michael joining in, giving them a thumbs down.

Thank you. I'm honored to be here with the amazing Jackson family and my beloved friend Michael who's kindness, generosity and caring for the world inspires millions. Michael is a remarkable human being with talent beyond comprehension, compassion beyond bounds and commitment to others beyond compare. Michael, we who know you more intimately than others acknowledge the suffering you have endured because we have suffered with you. But in the midst of our deepest anguish, we have known that you would prevail through this dark hour, that you would emerge stronger but still innocent, childlike, trusting, bruised but still magically untouched by the tongues and opinions of the world. Hurt, but still gloriously loving and benevolent despite the slings and arrows of those who know better. Enough of tabloid media! Enough of tabloid television! You know only you, the public, can accomplish this simply by not buying their garbage. Only you can put them out of business. Only you, and wouldn't that be great?! Michael, we know your recent torture isn't going to alter or change your compassion and love for children. There is beauty and truth in your being. You are the brightest star in the universe. Don't let anything dim your leading light. Neither crisis nor circumstances can ever take it away from you. And surely, Michael you still are 'The King of Pop' without a doubt. I love you so much Michael. Anyway, thank you all for honoring me for merely doing what I must do. Goodnight.

Taylor's declaration that Michael is still 'The King of Pop' brought a standing ovation from the audience. But as her speech continued the crowd grew eager to hear Michael sing and began chanting, "We want Michael!" and "Michael sing!" Taylor told the crowd, "I know you'd like to hear Michael sing, but he doesn't have any music prepared." Learning Michael would not be performing, some in the crowd began to call out in disappointment, "Oh! Oh!" which Taylor thought was booing, which she admonished, "Don't boo, it's an ugly sound." The crowd was clearly disappointed, but they did not boo Michael. The supposed booing was widely reported in the press before the show was broadcast no doubt costing the show many potential viewers, who decided to stick to watching the Olympics instead. Fans that attended the show strongly stressed the fact that they never booed Michael.

At the show's finale, Michael joined the rest of the family, and the other guests, on stage for "If Only You Believe". Janet was noticeably absent from the group. She had already left to rejoin her tour. She had taken the time out between two engagements to perform on the special but left immediately to go to the next stop on her janet. world tour. The family members took turns singing a few lines of the song. First Jermaine, followed by Rebbie, Randy, Marlon, Tito, and Jackie. Michael's first few words were nearly drowned out by the screams from the audience as he sang his allotted four lines of the song.

The crowd was ecstatic to see Michael Jackson in the flesh and cheered widely at each of his appearances. But while he was on stage for twenty five minutes, he did not sing, other than the four lines at the show's finale. And sing is what the audience paid up to $1,000 to see. Some would have paid even more. Carla Davenport, a fan from Pacifica, California, told one reporter, "I would pay $10,000, take out a loan, to see Michael perform. But we wanted to see him perform. They billed it as a Michael Jackson concert." The fans' disappointment at Michael not singing was widely reported before the show aired. *USA Today* ran the headline, "Jacksons No Thriller Without Michael Solo." The widely reported disappointment in the show undoubtedly cost the show valuable ratings points, and it came in third for the night. The Olympics, on CBS, attracted 36% of the viewing audience and came in first, the regular Tuesday night lineup on ABC came in second with 19% of the viewing audience, and NBC, with the *Jackson Family Honors*, attracted 17% of the viewing audience for third place. An upfront announcement of exactly what the fans could expect would have saved them being disappointed, rather than building expectations for something that could not be delivered.

The show's co-producer, Gary Smith, admitted it would have helped the show to have Michael perform but it wasn't in his control, "It would be a better show if he sang... but Michael is a unique artist and feels when he performs, it should be totally new and fresh. And he wasn't prepared to come in and do a totally new kind of performance." Michael's newly appointed publicist, Michael Levine, said, "It's a free country, people can speculate all they want... He was there to pay respects to people he loves. It wasn't his production."

Some reviewers of the show said the King of Pop blew his chance to remind his subjects why he warrants such royal treatment. The fans would certainly have loved to see Michael perform, but they in no way need reminding of what makes Michael so wonderful, so magical. They were simply mislead as to what to expect from the show. Print ads and television commercials hyping the special focused heavily, and sometimes exclusively, on Michael Jackson performing. Fans and viewers expected to see Michael Jackson perform.

Aside from the talk of the Jackson family reunion special, there was still more scandalous dirt to deliver, and *Hard Copy*, as always, was happy to dish it out. In another "exclusive" interview with yet another former security guard, which was stretched out to last for three shows, Diane Dimond talked with Charli Michaels, a former female security guard who worked at Neverland Valley. In the interview the former guard, who filed court documents in connection with the lawsuit filed by the other five former guards suing Michael, claimed she saw Michael touch the crotch of a young boy in a dance studio. She also claimed to have seen another boy in tears because Michael "had touched him funny." She went on to describe all of the "weird" or "questionable" circumstances she saw while working at the ranch. At the end of one part of the interview, Dimond added, "It must be said here that the two boys mentioned in this story have talked to police, they deny abuse occurred." This sentence, this very significant sentence which casts huge doubt on the guard's claims, took eight seconds for Dimond to say. Nice piece of balanced, objective reporting. This one part of the three part interview lasted eight minutes, the total interview lasted approximately twenty four minutes, while eight seconds was devoted to presenting the opposing side of the story.

The young boy Michaels said she saw Michael Jackson touch was Wade Robson. At the outbreak of the story of the allegations against Michael, ten year old Robson voluntarily told a Los Angeles TV station that he was friends with Michael and had spent time with him, but there was never any improper behavior by Michael, ever.

One of the claims the guard made was that the persona Michael Jackson portrays to the public is not the real Michael Jackson. She continued, saying that she could count the number of parties Michael hosted for children during her time at Neverland on one hand. Assuming she can count, and has the usual number of fingers, her statement is completely false. There have been numerous occasions on which Michael has invited groups of children to his ranch from various charities and organizations. Some of those have been mentioned here, many others are included in *Michael Jackson: The King of Pop*, published in 1993. Acknowledgement of these invitations have been made by the children who have visited the ranch, and by the many organizations which have recognized Michael's efforts in helping to bring happiness to children. Over the past several years Michael Jackson has worked with The Los Angeles YMCA, the Dream Street Program, the Make A Wish Foundation, the Boy Scouts of America, Big Brothers and Big Sisters, and many other organizations for children.

The roller coaster continued nonstop. Every time a new scandal was manufactured by the tabloid magazines or tabloid TV shows, someone else would step forward with support for Michael. This time it was Whitney Houston. In anticipation of her winning big at the Grammys, she was featured on the cover of the February 26, issue of *TV Guide*. In the accompanying interview she expressed her conviction that Michael should be assumed innocent until proven guilty, and she attacked the media for their persecution of him:

> *You do not convict someone of a crime that you have no idea he committed... This is something that was 'alleged': It has not been proven that Michael has done this. I hate the media for doing it to him. I really do. In*

the long run, in the United States of America, you're innocent until proven guilty. That's what I think stands. I just pray for Michael, and he knows he has my love.

Houston then questioned if the media bashing Michael had been subjected to was because he is black:

> *I see white folks do a lot of things I wouldn't even think of doing - and nobody cares. I think a lot of emphasis is placed on black people because there are not many who are able to succeed. So when one does, it's 'uh-oh'.*

While racism most certainly still exists, and to a much greater degree than we'd probably like to admit, the media attack on Michael Jackson never seemed to be race related. The media frenzy seemed to feed on the scent of blood and money, not color. One of the reasons his appeal is so massive is that he transcends the usual barriers of race, the barriers of age, and the barriers of sex. Michael Jackson is not regarded as the greatest black entertainer, but as the world's greatest entertainer, period. He appeals to people of all races, both sexes, and all ages. The media simply delights in tearing down anyone who will sell additional copies, or increase ratings. Certainly the recent scandals involving Mia Farrow and Woody Allen, Amy Fisher and Joey Buttafuoco, Burt Reynolds and Loni Anderson, Tonya Harding and Nancy Kerrigan, and Heidi Fleiss all suggest that the intense media bashing does not seem to be race related.

Disney officials for Epcot Center at Walt Disney World, reversing their statement made in November, announced on February 25, that they were replacing *Captain EO* at the Orlando, Florida theme park. They claimed it was not due to Michael's troubles and that plans had been in the works to replace the movie for eighteen months to keep everything fresh and new. They had no comment for why this planned replacement was not mentioned in November when they specifically stated they had no plans to replace *Captain EO*. A spokesman for Disney World said that the park was contacted by the press to see if the Jackson 3-D movie was being replaced. When they said yes, the press reported it as news and insinuated it was due to the allegations. According to a Disney spokesman, the 3-D movie was being pulled to be replaced in the fall with a 3-D movie with updated technology, *Honey, I Shrunk the Theater.*

While the alleged announcement, made some eighteen months earlier, that *Captain EO* was being replaced at Disney World seemed to be missed by virtually all of the media, it does seem that if the park were to pull the movie due to the allegations against Michael, they would have done so much earlier, and would not wait until fall to do so.

Disneyland in California, and in Tokyo, stated *Captain EO* continued as one of their most popular attractions and there were no plans to replace it at those locations.

Sega USA followed the lead of Pepsi and Disney World, and removed the likeness of Michael Jackson that had been featured as the host of a video ride in Las Vegas.

Another, yet dubious, supporter for Michael came in the form of the Nation of Islam leader, Louis Farrakhan. In a highly protested and controversial appearance on *Arsenio Hall*, Farrakhan, said Michael is being "treated like a slave on a plantation because of a charge that has yet to lead to a criminal charge." Farrakhan had earlier attended the taping of the *Jackson Family Honors.*

The grand jury in Santa Barbara questioned Joy Robson, the mother of Wade Robson, on March 1. This was probably due to the claims made by the former security guard who said she saw Michael touch the boy. Nothing of what was asked or what the witness, or any of the witnesses said, was revealed to the press.

Mid March was time again for the Los Angeles District Attorney to promise the investigation would be completed next month. Since the beginning of the case seven months earlier, it was going to be completed next month. First the D.A. predicted it would be done by mid October. October came and went and no end was in sight. So it was announced it would be completed next month, November. Then before the end of the year, December. Then early 1994, January. Then next month, February. There was no decision in February, or March. Gil Garcetti announced on March 15, that he expected a decision on whether or not to charge Michael in about six weeks. "In a month or so we will have the investigation wrapped up and within two to three weeks after that a decision will be made." So now it was going to be completed next month, April. Okay, maybe May. If they still didn't have any evidence by then to indict him, they could always delay it until June.

Meanwhile the criminal investigation continued. Katherine Jackson, having been subpoenaed two days earlier, testified before the grand jury in Los Angeles on March 17. She was accompanied by Randy. She was reportedly questioned about Michael's appearance in an attempt to determine if Michael had altered his appearance so it wouldn't match the description his accuser had given to police. When finished with her testimony, which took just over an hour, she refused questions from reporters but did issue one statement, "I'd just like to say that before I went I was sure of my son's innocence, now that I have finished my testimony, I still feel the same." It was leaked later that Katherine may have been asked which of her son's friends were gay. What relevance this had is anybody's guess.

Katherine's being subpoenaed to testify against her own son was highly unusual and it infuriated Katherine's attorney, Richard Steingard, Michael's attorneys, and most of all, Michael himself. Steingard told the press:

> *A prosecutor attempting or trying to use a mother against a son, a parent against a child is just wholly inappropriate and even more so inappropriate in this case because Mrs. Jackson has repeatedly and publicly denounced the allegations and insisted that her son was innocent.*
> *...I think there has to be a question whether there's an element of harassment, of the Jackson family, of attempting to divide them, to persecute them for a case that they can't make.*

Howard Weitzman was equally angered and frustrated:

> *...And now to try to humiliate Michael Jackson and harass him or his family by subpoenaing his mother seems to be to us the height of the indignity that the prosecutors could try to heap upon Michael.*
> *...if it was anybody but Michael Jackson, they wouldn't be spending our money, taxpayers money running around trying to create something that doesn't exist.*

Weitzman added,

> *In all the years of my experience, I've never before seen the mother of the target of an investigation called before the grand jury. It's just done in real poor taste. It borders on harassment.*

What is usually done in similar cases as this one however never seemed to apply here. From day one things did not go according to how they are usually done. Usually it must be shown that police have probable cause that a crime has been committed to obtain a search warrant, not just the unsubstantiated allegations of one person. Not in this case. Normally, a civil suit is not filed until a criminal investigation is complete. Not in this case, not with money being the primary objective. After exhausting all avenues of investigation and finding no evidence, the investigation is supposed to be completed with the conclusion that no crime was committed or that there is insufficient evidence to justify filing criminal charges. Not in this case, they just kept extending the investigation into more and more ludicrous directions.

If Michael Jackson happened not to be a superstar, it is very doubtful that the investigation would have lasted for so many months, if it was brought about at all. If he were Joe Average, it is very unlikely he would have been subjected to such scrutiny, spending untold amounts of taxpayers money questioning his friends, friends of friends, employees, or his mother, confiscating his medical records and conducting searches of each of his homes, and his body. Some felt Michael Jackson bought himself out of trouble with his millions. It could very well be argued he was only in the situation because of his millions, and his wealth bought him undue scrutiny.

The order for his mother to testify before the grand jury seemed to infuriate and hurt Michael more than anyone. He immediately issued a public statement condemning the Los Angeles District Attorney's office:

For the purposes of headline grabbing, the L.A. District Attorney's office continues to persecute me and this has now expanded to include the harassment of my beloved mother.

Two days before Katherine Jackson appeared before the grand jury, it was reported that Marlon Brando had been ordered to testify. It was reported that Brando spent three hours being questioned about whether or not his son Miko had ever discussed the case with him. Brando's attorney, Edward Medvene, issued a statement denying Brando had ever been subpoenaed to testify, "Mr. Brando asked us to convey to you his denial... that, on Tuesday of this week, he appeared before the ... grand jury concerning the investigation of Michael Jackson."

At this time a petition was filed of several Santa Barbara Grand Jury witnesses requesting a gag order be lifted. An order had been placed on the witnesses up to this point prohibiting them from speaking about any of the proceedings. The petition asked that the court "... to cease and desist from permitting the grand jury of Santa Barbara County to admonish grand jury witnesses to keep secret, or require an oath of secrecy from them." The petition charged Santa Barbara County prosecutors with brow beating and intimidating witnesses appearing before the grand jury.

Anthony Pellicano appeared before the Santa Barbara Grand Jury on March 21. He answered questions for three hours in an effort by the grand jury to determine if he had obstructed justice, altered evidence, or influenced witnesses.

On March 19, the Heroes, Legends, Superstars of Hollywood and Rock auction was staged by Beverly Hills' Superior Auction Gallery and Startifacts. The most talked about of the items going up for auction were a handful of handwritten notes from Michael Jackson, one of which read, "Candy, all the video tapes I gave you, If you can't put them in our vault, then give them all to Lee Tucker. Do not have them out like you have them. Send them to Lee's today." Another piece of paper from Michael contained a depressing poem, "I start to givin' up. Life is an agrivator (sic). The bills are pillin' up... This stuff ain't good for me." These notes were now given a second look for some hidden significance in light of his recent troubles.

Michael was meanwhile getting back to work. He had reportedly resurrected an earlier project. He was to have contributed a song to the *Addams Family Values* soundtrack. That song, "Is This Scary" was now being finished along with an extended length video. The video, financed by Michael, was said to cost $6 million.

Leading up to the Oscar telecast on March 21, Barbara Walters held her annual interview special. One of her three interviewees this year was Elton John, who spoke candidly about his homosexuality, his dependency problems, and his efforts to help someone else with their dependency problems, Michael Jackson. He confirmed once again that Michael was indeed having problems with addiction, that he help put Michael in touch with a therapist:

He was fragile. I know for a fact that he'd been mum about the amount of painkillers people had been giving him and stuff like that. And I know it wasn't a case of running out of the country for an excuse, he had a real problem.

Elton also described Michael's condition when he first arrived in Britain:

He was like a zombie. And that's how he arrived in this country, a zombie. It takes a while to get over that and he's gone right back into that mayhem situation over there. I fear for him.

Elton offered Michael encouragement, and was glad the press wasn't able to track Michael to his house during his stay there. But he did disagree with his decision to settle the civil lawsuit, despite admitting he knew none of the facts of the case:

I wouldn't have settled. And I wouldn't care if I had to sell my last thing in life just to clear my name. I don't know anything about Michael Jackson's case whatsoever, I don't know any of the facts. I know if I had been innocent I would have said, 'I'm going for it'.

While the various lawsuits against Michael continued, he had a lawsuit against a British tabloid to contend with as well as a pending case against a former photographer. The *Daily Mirror*, a British tabloid, ran a story in 1992 in which they said Michael's face was badly scarred, and was falling apart due to the extensive plastic surgeries he has had. Michael filed suit against the tabloid. In March, 1994 a British judge ruled that in order to pursue his case, Michael would have to undergo a facial examination and supply his medial records. They would have to take a number, because first, Michael would have to try and get them back from the investigators in Los Angeles, it seemed everybody wanted his medical records. The exam, it was stipulated, must take place in proper lighting conditions.

Michael's lawsuit against Steve Howell, a former photographer, was set for March 29. Michael was suing Howell for selling video tapes of Michael without his permission. Michael was requesting the tapes be returned and $250,000 in damages. The video tapes being sold showed Michael, in 1984, being interviewed on the grounds of his Encino home. The quality of the video is very poor.

On March 22, 1994, a hearing was held concerning the request of Michael's attorneys for the return of the photos taken during the body search. They also asked for a full copy of the affidavit used to obtain the warrant on Michael Jackson's body. His attorney's had previously been given a readapted version, with portions of the affidavit blocked out. A decision on the matter was postponed until April 11. Meanwhile the photos were being held in a safe deposit box in a Santa Barbara bank. Two signatures of high ranking officials were required to remove the photos. The request was denied.

A renewed request for the return of the photos was made by Michael's lawyers on May 10. They argued the body search was unconstitutional and that it made Michael hysterical. Thomas Sneddon argued that Michael was not naked during the search, that he wore swimming trunks and two robes, and that the search was done in sections, as if that made some difference.

Superior Court Judge James Slater postponed any decision until "later".

Even more legal troubles loomed for Michael and the Jackson family. Gary Smith, of Smith-Hemion, co-producer of the *Jackson Family Honors* filed a lawsuit on March 31 for $2.2 million against the Jackson family for nonpayment of the cast and crew of the show. Included in the $2.2 million was Smith's fee of $400,000. Instead of the projected profits of $6 million, the special was estimated to have lost $1.7 million. Jermaine, the show's co-producer, said, "While the final amount of the loss is not completely known, it is our intention that all creditors will eventually be fully paid." It was reported that of the $4.5 million in total revenue, only $100,00 was being distributed to charity.

Specifically, the lawsuit named Jackson Communications, Inc., Jackson Jubilee Inc., Transworld International, Ticketmaster - Las Vegas Inc., Ticketmaster of Delaware Valley, Michael Jackson, Janet Jackson, Jermaine Jackson, Jackie Jackson, Randy Jackson, Tito Jackson, Joseph Jackson, Katherine Jackson, Rebbie Jackson, and Marlon Jackson. The complaints included breach of contract; breach of the implied covenant of good faith and fair dealing; bad faith denial of the existence of the contract, conversion, negligence, and fraud. Despite the long list of defendants, the complaint put a good deal of the blame on only one person, Michael Jackson, saying they had relied on Michael Jackson performing on the show to make it a success, "Smith-Hemion relied upon that commitment in determining to enter into the production agreement."

While Smith may have realized that because the show lost money, the Jacksons may have some difficulty in meeting their financial obligations, he was fully aware there were some members of the family who could definitely afford it. Fred Richman, Smith's attorney, said, "The family may not have money, but Michael and Janet do."

Indeed, at the time the suit was filed, Tito and Jermaine were in Farmington Hills, Michigan, taping their second commercial for car dealer Mel Farr. Farr, who owns dealerships in Michigan and Ohio, gave Tito and Jermaine each a Lincoln Town Car for their participation. Tito and Jermaine had first appeared in ads for the car dealer in 1992.

Michael was at this time touring mansions in Newport, Rhode Island. He toured The Breakers, The Elms, Marble House, Rosecliff, and Kingscote, asking if any of them were for sale. He had earlier toured the Egyptian and American wings of the Metropolitan Museum of Art. His visit was arranged for after hours.

Garth Brooks and Wynona were probably not exactly shaking in their cowboy boots when it was reported that LaToya Jackson was in Nashville recording her debut Country album. Despite not being signed to any recording contract, Jack Gordon predicted, "She will be the new Country Western heartthrob."

At the National Figure Skating Salute, a skating exhibition held on April 9, the Korean national champion, Lily Lee, skated to Michael Jackson's music. She skated to "Heal the World" and "Jam". It was reminiscent of German champion and Olympic gold medalist, Katerina Witt's salute to Michael Jackson during the 1988 Olympic exhibition where she skated to "Bad". Just a couple of weeks later the Fox network aired a figure skating special which featured rock 'n roll music. Russian gold medalist Oksana Baiul skated to "In The Closet". In talking about her choice of music she said

"My favorite is Michael Jackson. I love the way Michael moves."

A Santa Barbara judge extended the term of the Santa Barbara Grand Jury on April 11, which had reached the end of its ninety day term. In commenting on the extension, Howard Weitzman said, "I think this investigation is moving forward so that the district attorney's office can look for additional (evidence) that I don't believe exists out there."

Contrary to the extension of the Santa Barbara grand jury, many reports maintained that the criminal investigations of Michael Jackson by the Los Angeles County District Attorney and the Santa Barbara County District Attorney were completed and there was no evidence to support filing criminal charges against Michael Jackson. Sources from the police department told the media the investigators on the case had been reassigned to other cases and they were no longer actively pursuing the criminal investigation of Michael Jackson. Jordy Chandler was not cooperating with the grand jury, so not only did they not have sufficient evidence that a crime was committed, they no longer had an alleged victim. According to these reports, the case would technically remain open for the duration of the statute of limitations, six years, in case the boy ever changed his mind and decided to cooperate with prosecutors.

Both district attorneys denied these reports. Gil Garcetti said the investigation was continuing but they did expect to have it completed very soon and they expected to make an announcement by the end of the month. Tom Sneddon also denied the investigation was completed and said prosecutors hoped to talk with the boy in the coming week. The week came and went without the boy talking to anyone.

The investigation couldn't be over soon enough for many of Michael's fans, one in particular. Denise Pfeiffer, a twenty four year old British fan flew to California from England where she was later arrested and charged with vandalizing the office of a certain Beverly Hills dentist. Pfeiffer, who had spray painted the sidewalk outside Chandler's office, stole his bathroom key, and had made telephone calls to Chandler, was charged with vandalism, misdemeanor petty theft and making obscene telephone calls. Pfieffer is a contributing writer to *Off The Wall* magazine, an all-Jackson magazine published in England.

Michael wasn't wasting any time getting on with his life. He was reportedly working on the much talked about and ever delayed greatest hits album, now scheduled for release in the fall, and he was said to be working on new songs for a new album, the release date of which had not yet been set. Michael was also involved in developing a musical remake of the fantasy movie, *The Seven Faces of Dr. Lao*, which was originally released in 1964.

An invitation to Michael to present an award at the 1994 World Music Awards was extended by the show's executive producer Gary Pudney. Michael, 1993's biggest winner, did not attend.

Michael was said to be looking at a new home. This one in Florida, ten minutes from Walt Disney World in Orlando. The massive house was set on an immense piece of property and cost approximately $10 million. It was said Michael was interested in building a park on the property for children. There were no reports he was interested in selling Neverland, though he couldn't be blamed for wanting to leave California.

While Michael was getting on with his life, the Los Angeles and Santa Barbara County prosecutors refused to end the criminal investigations against him. As April came to a close, their announced deadline for a decision, there came a public statement saying just the opposite. Contrary to what he had said a couple of weeks earlier, but right in keeping with his track record, Gil Garcetti announced, "The investigation is continuing and there is no estimate as to when it will be concluded." They were reportedly having trouble sorting through the testimony of the two grand juries 110 miles apart. Why it was necessary to review the testimony again is a mystery as it had been revealed by one of the jurors that they had heard no damaging testimony against Michael.

Just a few days later it was announced that the grand jury in Santa Barbara county had disbanded. The grand jury, after spending more than three months hearing the case, was never called upon to render a decision in the case. The district attorney had never asked the grand jury to indict him, the grand jury was said to have been formed for information gathering purposes only. Michael's attorneys said the jury was disbanded because there was no evidence for them to consider. While the grand jury was disbanded the investigation still remained open in both counties. It is difficult to say how much longer they could draw it out as they had no evidence to ponder, and no alleged victim. The possibility remained however that a second grand jury could be impaneled in Santa Barbara.

In an outstanding show of support for Michael Jackson, and as an indication of how much his fans and the public believe in him, Michael Jackson was honored as "a person who cares most about kids." The Caring for Kids Award was awarded to Michael Jackson at New York's City Center on April 28. In a survey of 100,000 children, ages eight to sixteen, from New York, New Jersey and Connecticut, over 750,000 voted Michael Jackson as the person who cares most about children. The award is sponsored by Body Sculpt, a non-profit group that uses physical fitness to discourage kids from using drugs. Body Sculpt president, Vincent Ferguson, said the allegations against Michael Jackson didn't bother him one bit, "And it doesn't bother the children."

Michael seemed very proud and happy in accepting the honor. Having never been much of a clothes horse, he was dressed in the same black and gold jacket he had worn at the *Jackson Family Honors*. Surrounded by children on the stage, he read from a prepared statement thanking the children for the honor.

Michael was clearly not letting the continuing investigation to overwhelm him or interfere with his work. As usual, he was juggling a number of projects at one time, and was seeming to enjoy his personal life as well, knowing in his heart he is innocent of any wrongdoing. Michael will undoubtedly continue to dominate the music charts throughout the nineties as he did throughout the eighties. His upcoming albums will be especially eagerly anticipated to see how he artistically expresses the incredible pain and suffering he has had to endure for several very long months.

Despite the continuing investigations, Michael Jackson and Michaelmania seemed to be getting gradually back to normal. May 14 and 15 MTV was once again given over to Michael and Janet Jackson. Videos, specials, and Rockumentaries on the talented Jackson siblings dominated the music networks programming for the weekend.

For the second time in the young year, Michael Jackson was featured on the cover of another premiere issue of a magazine. *People Today*, in its July, 1994 issue, offered a review of Michael's life and addressed the allegations he now faced. The issue presented responses from a random sampling of interviews done with people on the streets of New York. Nineteen of these responses were printed in the issue. Not one of which felt Michael Jackson was guilty of any wrongdoing. Not one person felt there has been any evidence uncovered to suggest Michael was capable of such behavior. Not one. There were plenty of people however who expressed their belief that Michael was the true victim and that money was at the root of the allegations being made and the longevity of the allegations in the media. Person after person expressed their faith in Michael and their continued admiration.

The *People Today* issue explored the allegations against Michael and their most probable cause, money:

Mr. Jackson has shown us time and time again... he actually cares! That factor alone, leads loyal fans and Jackson Watchers to doubt allegations. Especially allegations that could be so very financially profitable for the accusing parties.

... 'If Michael Jackson WAS guilty, this whole matter would have never come up in the media and press,' said a New York City P.I. in response to our request for an opinion. 'A suitcase full of cash would have quietly changed hands in some airport lavatory, and the matter would have dissolved. The very fact that you and I are

hearing about it, means to me, that Mr. Jackson is out-raged and has decided to confront the allegations directly. Only an innocent man would chose such a direction. Especially with so many eyes looking in his direction. For that matter, only an innocent man would be outraged!'

Contrary to what his accusers had hoped, Michael Jackson will prevail. Some people tend to see Michael as being weak and fragile but actually he is strong and determined. Throughout this eight months of hell he has consistently and without exception proved his skeptics wrong. He has maintained the love, admiration and respect of his millions of fans throughout the world and he has maintained a level of integrity others could-n't hope to match.

Certainly Michael cannot come out of this situation without being strongly affected by it. Learning that people will, without hesitation, turn on him for profit will certainly deepen his distrust of others. Hopefully his love and trust of children won't be damp-ened, for Michael seems to derive the most joy from being with children.

Besides taking an emotional toll, the allegations made against Michael Jackson, the media's massacre of him, and the seemingly unending investigations, also took a physical toll. Sleepless nights, loss of appetite, migraine headaches, stress and depression were not uncommon. And, as described here, it also had physical effects on Michael!

Michael Jackson has displayed dignity, strength of moral character and integrity that should be an inspiration to all. Michael Jackson is unquestionably the greatest entertainer in the world. He is also the world's finest humanitarian. He has only ever wanted to make people happy and help make the world a better place, and he has done that time and time again. He is The King of Pop.

> *In our darkest hour*
> *In my deepest despair*
> *Will you still care?*
> *Will you be there?*

Yes, Michael.

Lisa Campbell
Flint, Michigan
1994

1. Originally selling for $2.99, Michael Raisin, a California Raisin figure modeled after Michael Jackson, was listed in toy collector magazines in 1993 as being worth $35 to $100. Michael Raisin is the rarest of the California Raisin collectibles.

2. The June, 1993, issue of *Life* magazine gave a first time look at Neverland Valley.

3. Michael Jackson shared the cover of the June, 1993, issue of *Disney Adventures* magazine with Pinocchio. The issue offered "25 Things You (Probably) Didn't Know About Michael Jackson".

4. News of the allegations being made against Michael Jackson dominated the media for months.

5. Some publications continued to focus on Michael Jackson's proven talents and humanitarianism rather than rumors, scandal, and lies.

6. Sales of *Dangerous* were not affected by the news of the allegations against Michael Jackson. In fact several outlets reported an *increase* in sales.

7. Sony bet Michaelmania was alive and well, and they won. *Dangerous: The Short Films,* released in November, 1993, spent its first six months of release in the top ten of *Billboard's* Top Music Videos, with no sign of dropping out any time soon.

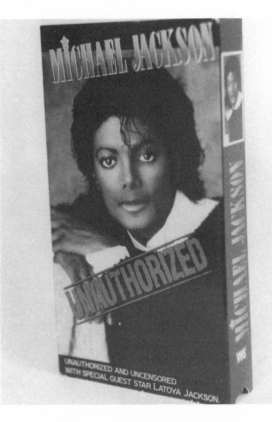

8. *Michael Jackson: Unauthorized* prompted a lawsuit from Michael against a former photographer for selling poor quality, unauthorized, video tapes taken ten years earlier.